The Gluten-Free, Hassle-Free Cookbook

Also by Marlisa Brown, MS, RD, CDE, CDN

Gluten-Free, Hassle-Free, Second Edition

American Dietetic Association Easy Gluten-Free (with Tricia Thompson, MS, RD)

The Gluten-Free, Hassle-Free Cookbook

Delicious, Foolproof Recipes for
Every Day and Every Occasion

Marlisa Brown, MS, RD, CDE, CDN

Food Styling and Photography by Marlisa Brown

Visit our website at www.demoshealth.com

ISBN: 978-1-936303-79-3
e-book ISBN: 978-1-61705-232-3

Acquisitions Editor: Julia Pastore
Compositor: DiacriTech

Medical information provided by Demos Health, in the absence of a visit with a health care professional, must be considered as an educational service only. This book is not designed to replace a physician's independent judgment about the appropriateness or risks of a procedure or therapy for a given patient. Our purpose is to provide you with information that will help you make your own health care decisions.

The information and opinions provided here are believed to be accurate and sound, based on the best judgment available to the authors, editors, and publisher, but readers who fail to consult appropriate health authorities assume the risk of injuries. The publisher is not responsible for errors or omissions. The editors and publisher welcome any reader to report to the publisher any discrepancies or inaccuracies noticed.

Library of Congress Cataloging-in-Publication Data
Brown, Marlisa.
  The gluten-free, hassle-free cookbook: delicious, foolproof recipes for every day and every occasion / Marlisa Brown MS, RD, CDE, CDN; food styling and photography by Marlisa Brown.
    pages cm
  Includes bibliographical references and index.
  ISBN 978-1-936303-79-3 — ISBN 978-1-61705-232-3 (e-book)
  1. Gluten-free diet—Recipes. 2. Celiac disease—Diet therapy—Recipes. I. Title.
  RM237.86.B7593 2015
  641.5′638—dc23
                          2015000346

Special discounts on bulk quantities of Demos Health books are available to corporations, professional associations, pharmaceutical companies, health care organizations, and other qualifying groups. For details, please contact:

Special Sales Department
Demos Medical Publishing, LLC
11 West 42nd Street, 15th Floor
New York, NY 10036
Phone: 800-532-8663 or 212-683-0072
Fax: 212-941-7842
E-mail: specialsales@demosmedical.com

Printed in the United States of America by Bang Printing.
15 16 17 18 19 / 5 4 3 2 1

In loving memory

To my mother, Ann Brown, who always entertained with style.

To my aunt, Gracie Hart, whose home was the central point for our family holidays.

To my grandma Ruthie Metli, the heart of our family. Separated from her siblings and extended family as a teenager, she was always happiest when we were together and she would share her holiday toast:

"Our family should always be together, and we should be happy and healthy."

Mom, Grandma, and Aunt Gracie

Contents

Acknowledgments

I could not have completed this collection of delicious gluten-free recipes without the support of the wonderful people who made my work truly a pleasure.

- Catherine Brittan, MS, RD, for her brilliant contributions in testing, analyzing, and working on many of these recipes.

- My sister-in-law, Rosemarie Kass, for her fabulous, tried-and-true family recipes that were so easily modified to make them gluten free.

- My husband, Russell Schimmenti, for his endless tastings.

- My aunt, Ann Metli, chef Chris Singlemann from Watermill Caterers, and my sister-in-law Eileen Ciaccio, who contributed recipes.

- My agent, Stephany Evans, who has always been there for me as a source of encouragement and support and without whom I could not have completed this book.

- And finally, a thank you to my team at Demos Health, especially Julia Pastore, for working together with me to put out such a truly wonderful book.

Introduction

I have always been drawn to the world of food: cooking it, growing it, and learning about cooking techniques and favorite recipes. When you love to cook or love to eat, omitting any common ingredient such as gluten can feel like a struggle. It did for me when I first went gluten free in 2008, after I discovered I had non-celiac gluten sensitivity. Even as a registered dietitian and nutritional consultant, I was initially overwhelmed by the changes I needed to make. But then I got to work! I rolled up my sleeves, put on my cooking apron, pulled out my recipes, and with some trial and error (OK, lots of error in the beginning) discovered that living gluten free doesn't have to be frustrating, time consuming, expensive—or tasteless! With some simple adjustments and tried-and-true tricks of the trade you can eat all of your favorite foods, including some that you may have thought were a distant memory, such as fresh pasta, flaky breads, and moist cakes.

In this cookbook, I'd like to share with you the recipes I come back to again and again, as I hope you will, too. As a dietitian, I work with many clients who follow a gluten-free diet. Without fail, each client asks for more recipes for classic comfort foods and traditional holiday favorites. Food is at the heart of so many special occasions, and I understand what it's like to feel left out. I wrote this book in order to share those recipes with you, especially my personal favorites.

These recipes are made with easily accessible ingredients and packed with flavor, making any meal special. You'll find quick weeknight dinners such as chicken parmesan and grilled salmon with balsamic glaze, comfort food classics such as mac and cheese and pizza, kid-friendly snacks and appetizers such as pigs in a blanket, garlic knots, and zucchini sticks, and lots of decadent desserts (is my sweet tooth showing?) such as rocky road, black and white cookies, and chocolate peanut butter tart.

Many of my recipes are simple and take minimal prep and cooking time, but when you're really in a pinch, look for my recipes labeled "quick and easy," which can be made in 30 minutes or less. Some of my recipes may take a little longer, such as my homemade pasta or crusty French bread (yes, I said "crusty"), but they're worth it—I promise. I've also kept an eye on the fat content in these recipes. It is important to make low-fat choices whenever possible because gluten-free packaged foods are often loaded with added fats.

For those of you who may have more than one food allergy or intolerance or are following a vegetarian, vegan, or low-FODMAP diet, I've included other top allergen information for each recipe and included substitutions where possible to accommodate these restrictions. Always make sure ingredient substitutions are free of all of your food allergens or intolerances.

I have made every effort to accurately note food allergens, but since companies often change ingredients, please be sure to always check food labels or to contact the manufacturer to confirm that a food is safe for you.

GF = gluten free: All recipes in this book are gluten free.

MF = milk free: Does not contain milk products or any milk-containing ingredient.

EF = egg free: Does not contain eggs or any egg-containing ingredient.

SF = soy free: does not contain soy or any soy-containing ingredient.

NF = nut free: does not contain any tree nuts. (See note on coconut.)

PF = peanut free: does not contain any peanuts or peanut-containing ingredient.

FF = fish free: does not contain any finfish or fish-containing ingredient.

SFF = shellfish free: does not contain any shellfish or shellfish-containing ingredient.

V = vegetarian: does not contain meat, poultry, or fish; it may contain milk or eggs.

VG = vegan: does not contain any animal product, including milk, eggs, or honey.

A note on coconut: Coconut is not a botanical nut and is not treated as a nut in this book; it is classified as a fruit, even though the Food and Drug Administration recognizes coconut as a tree nut. Although allergic reactions to coconut have been documented, most people who are allergic to tree nuts can safely eat coconut. If you are allergic to tree nuts, talk to your allergist before adding coconut to your diet.

What is a low-FODMAP diet?

FODMAP is an acronym for Fermentable, Oligo-, Di- and Mono-saccharides and Polyols, used to describe a group of fermentable short-chain carbohydrates. Reducing the intake of FODMAPs may provide relief for people with irritable bowel syndrome (IBS) and other functional gut disorders.

Foods high in FODMAPs fall into five main categories. I've included only a sample of foods in each category. For a complete list and help crafting a low-FODMAP diet, speak with a registered dietitian who specializes in low-FODMAP diets.

Foods high in FODMAPs:

Lactose: milk, yogurt, ice cream, and certain cheeses

Fructose: fruits such as apples, pears, and peaches, as well as coconut milk, dried fruits, agave, and honey

Fructans: vegetables such as artichokes, Brussels sprouts, broccoli, onions, and garlic

Galactans: such as lentils, kidney beans, and soy products

Polyols: fruits such as blackberries, cherries, and watermelon

Meet the members of my family who have shared so many of my gluten-free recipes during holidays and celebrations. As my grandmother used to say, "Happy and Healthy." From my family to yours—Enjoy!

Marlisa

Getting Started Cooking Gluten Free

You may be following a gluten-free diet because you have celiac disease, non-celiac gluten sensitivity, or are sensitive to FODMAPs. Or you may just feel better going gluten free. Whatever your reasons for following a gluten-free diet, it is important to find ways to make gluten-free living fit easily into your lifestyle.

Gluten is a protein that is found in wheat, rye, and barley. It is often found in baked goods, cereals, and desserts, and is used as a thickener in gravies and soups, as a coating, and as a flavoring agent (in malted products); it is also used in many packaged foods. Gluten can be hidden in broths, dips, condiments, imitation crabmeat, beer, hot dogs, soy sauce, and coated nuts, to name just a few possibilities. This may sound like a lot to be on the lookout for, but there are many gluten-free options available and most fresh foods are naturally gluten free. Here are some helpful guidelines for choosing gluten-free foods and ingredients:

Alcohol: All distilled alcohols (such as vodka, gin, and scotch) are considered gluten free. (The distillation process removes the gluten, but these products most likely will not be labeled gluten free. Note, however, that distilled alcohol products sometimes have flavoring agents added after distillation that could contain gluten). Beer is not distilled and is made from barley, so it is not gluten free. There are many gluten-free beers now being produced, but some brands may be safer than others and you should do some research before making your selections. Wine is considered gluten free although some red wines have used wheat flour to seal the barrels—to date, wines tested have shown gluten content to be within the safe range of less than 20 parts per million. It is hoped that as they improve testing methods in the future, it will be easier for all to safely select alcoholic beverages.

Beans, Tofu, and Soy: Beans are gluten free and high in fiber, but on rare occasions gluten may be added to flavored beans. To be safe, buy canned or dried plain, unseasoned beans, or check the packaging to make sure no gluten-containing ingredient has been added. Tofu is also gluten free, unless it is baked or marinated in a gluten-containing ingredient such as soy sauce. Most soy-based food products are gluten free, except those marinated in a wheat-containing ingredient or those with added barley malt or fillers. Soy sauce is usually made from wheat, and cannot be used; however, there are some gluten-free varieties of soy sauce available.

Cereal: Most store-brand cereals contain gluten. Though you can now find some cereals in the supermarket that are safe to eat (such as Rice Chex, Corn Chex, Honey Nut Chex, Chocolate Chex, Cinnamon Chex, grits, Cream of Rice, Nature's Path Mesa Sunrise cereal, and Bakery on Main Street products), in general, most gluten-free cereals will be found in specialty and health food stores.

Cheese: Real cheeses are gluten free (unless gluten-containing ingredients are added, as is sometimes the case with blends and cheese spreads or if marinated in beer). Note, too, that shredded cheese may have gluten-containing anticaking agents.

Chips (Potato and Corn): Most brands that are made from corn or potato with only oil and salt added are gluten free. When unsure, pick unflavored chips, which are much less likely to contain gluten. If you make your own potato and corn chips, be sure to use a dedicated gluten-free fryer to prevent cross-contamination.

Cold Cuts: Gluten-free choices are available from many brands such as Boar's Head, Hillshire Farms, Hormel, and Wellshire Farms. When you are uncertain, it is safest to pick pure meats that are 100% meat, such as real roasted turkey or roast beef, with no added fillers. Always ask if it is possible for the slicing machine to be wiped down prior to having your cold cuts sliced, since you cannot be sure if gluten-containing products have been sliced previously on that equipment. You also need to ask your server to use a new pair of gloves.

Corn Tortillas: Most brands are gluten free, but, again, read the labels to make sure there are no added ingredients. If the label says corn, salt, and oil and there is no warning about possible wheat contamination, corn tortillas are usually safe to use.

Dairy Products: Usually gluten free. Milk, half-and-half, cream cheese, cottage cheese (in rare instances, gluten is added), butter, and ricotta cheese are naturally gluten free. Processed cheese blends, some light sour creams, and, occasionally, flavored yogurts and other flavored dairy products may contain gluten.

Desserts: Most whipped toppings and egg custards are gluten free, except those with cookie dough or toppings mixed in (check labels for added fillers). Some examples of gluten-free dessert mixes include those sold by Pamela's Products, 1-2-3 Gluten-Free, and Bob's Red Mill.

Eggs: All eggs and egg whites, as well as most egg substitutes, are gluten free.

Fish: All fresh fish is gluten free, unless it is breaded or flavored with a gluten-containing marinade. Be careful though, because fresh fish displayed in the same case as breaded fish may be cross-contaminated. Imitation shellfish, such as crab sticks, often contains gluten.

Gluten-Free Flours, Grains, and Starches: There are many grains and flours that are naturally gluten free, such as almond meal, amaranth, bean, buckwheat, coconut, cornmeal, grits, millet, gluten-free oats, potato, quinoa, rice, sorghum, and teff flours. Please be careful if flavoring agents or fillers are added, as they may contain gluten; also be on your guard for possible cross-contamination during the grain manufacturing processes. When in doubt, look for products labeled gluten free. Note that gluten-free grains can be contaminated at point of sale or in transport, especially those weighed and bagged in health food stores.

Fresh potatoes are always gluten free, and 100% pure potato starch or flakes are safe. One gluten-free grain easily found in supermarkets is rice, which is available in a number of varieties: brown, jasmine, instant, long-grain, and so forth. However, unless labeled as gluten free, avoid supermarket rice blends such as Rice-a-Roni and similar products, which are often seasoned with gluten-containing ingredients. Always check with the manufacturers if in doubt.

Ice Cream: Most ice cream and gelato is gluten free, but it is important to check the labels to make sure that no cookies, wafers, chips, sprinkles, wheat, or barley malt have been added. Be careful of cross-contamination in ice cream parlors where the ice cream scoop may have touched a cone or been used to serve ice cream with cookie dough or other gluten-containing ingredients.

Ices: Almost all ices and sorbets are gluten free, but don't buy ices that have crunchies, sprinkles, or cookie dough folded in. When in doubt, look for gluten free on the label or check the ingredients to make sure there is no added wheat or barley malt.

Meats and Poultry: Most pure meats are gluten free, except those that are breaded or marinated in a gluten-containing mixture. Poultry that has a self-basting agent or broth added usually contains gluten. Make sure you use 100% pure poultry, beef, and pork to be safe. Look for those that have no additives listed in the ingredients. If you want to marinate foods, do so yourself and use gluten-free marinades and dressings.

Nuts and Oils: Almost all nuts and vegetable oils are gluten free unless the nuts are coated with a flavoring agent or processed on equipment that has also processed wheat. Butter, margarine, and shortening are also gluten free as long as they have not been cross-contaminated.

Oats: In the past, it was thought that those following a gluten-free diet could not consume oats, even though pure oats do not contain gluten. Recent evidence has shown that if oats are grown and processed so that they do not get contaminated with gluten, they should be safe for many who are following a gluten-free diet. When using oats, make sure they are from a gluten-free source and clearly state that they are certified gluten free.

Popcorn: Air-popped fresh popcorn using fresh kernels is gluten free. Flavored popcorn can contain gluten, so it is important to double-check each brand for safety.

Produce: Fresh fruits and vegetables are all gluten free, and frozen and canned fruits and vegetables are usually gluten free unless additives, coatings, sauces, or fillers that contain gluten are used. Dried fruits and fruit juices are also usually gluten free. On occasion, dried flavored fruits or dates may have been dusted with flour (to prevent sticking), so look for 100% pure dried fruit.

Pudding: Most puddings are gluten free.

Rice Cakes: Check labels as some varieties contain gluten.

Salad Dressings: Many salad dressings are gluten free, but some brands may add fillers or barley malt, so care should be taken. Try the dressing I drizzle over my beef and spinach salad on page 50 instead.

Sauces, Dressings, and Marinades: Many gluten-free choices are available; look for brands that are labeled gluten free or those that have been checked for gluten-free status. Or make your own creamy cilantro pesto (page 106), spicy mustard sauce (page 123), or marinara sauce (page 117).

Seasonings: Fresh and dried herbs, all whole spices, and garlic and onion powder are gluten free and are safe. Seasoning blends may include a gluten-containing filler, so do not use these unless they are labeled gluten free or you have checked with the manufacturer first.

Soy Milk: If you are lactose intolerant, you may be using lactaid milk or soy milk. There are some gluten-free brands of soy milk such as Silk, Trader Joe's, and WestSoy, but double-check other brands for gluten—sometimes gluten is added as barley malt.

Sweeteners: Almost all sweeteners are gluten free, including sugar, Sweet 'n' Low, Equal, Splenda, Stevia, agave, honey, molasses, and many more. Barley malt is not gluten free.

Vinegars: All distilled vinegars are gluten free. Vinegars that may contain gluten include malt vinegars and those made with barley, such as rice vinegar (rice vinegar is not distilled and sometimes includes barley).

Yogurts: Most popular brands are gluten free, but always check the label and do not select yogurt with sprinkles or candy toppings.

Putting Together a Gluten-Free Pantry

I always keep the following staples on hand. Keep gluten-free grains and flours fresh longer by storing them in the refrigerator. Gluten-free bread goes bad quickly, so I keep it (and bread crumbs) in the freezer. Sometimes I wrap and store gluten-free desserts in the freezer and defrost in the microwave for about 10 seconds when I want something sweet. The only gluten-free items I actually store in my pantry are cereals, crackers, canned goods, and jarred products.

- Gluten-free pasta
- One or more gluten-free grains such as rice, quinoa, or buckwheat
- Gluten-free cereal such as Rice Chex (It's great for breakfast, but also can be used to make a crust, coating, or topping)
- Gluten-free all-purpose flour blend
- Gluten-free bread, rolls, and bread crumbs
- Garlic and onion powder
- Fresh herbs and spices
- Leavening agents such as xanthan gum, baking soda, and baking powder
- Seltzer, vinegar, gelatin, nut butters, and fruit purees (these help to create better texture when baking without gluten)
- Pure almond and vanilla extract and cocoa powder as flavoring agents
- Gluten-free chocolate

Working with Gluten-Free Flours, Starches, and Leavening Agents

Learning how to work with gluten-free flours, starches, and leavening agents will enable you to create substitutes for your favorite traditionally gluten-filled foods and add new flavors to your meals. Except for baked goods, most gluten-free flours can be used in place of all-purpose flour in many recipes, including as a thickening agent for sauces and a coating for fried foods. It gets a bit trickier when baking, as you'll need a blend to create a light, airy texture. If you baked bread using just one grain, such as rice flour, it would be heavy, dense, and crumbly and would easily fall apart—in short, inedible.

I'll tell you more about flour blends in the next section, but for now here are some of the most commonly used gluten-free flours, starches, and leavening agents:

Amaranth Flour: This is one of the ancient grains. I like using amaranth flour when I am trying to lighten up a gluten-free flour blend as it has more health benefits than the starches often used, and it is high in iron and fiber.

Arrowroot Flour: This is a starch that can be used at equal amounts to replace cornstarch in recipes and is a great alternative for those who cannot have corn.

Bean Flours: High-protein flours like bean flours can provide a better texture to baking blends. Try them in desserts, breads, and homemade pasta blends. Since some people are allergic to beans, it is always important to let others know when you include them in your recipes. Bean flours are nutrient rich and high in B vitamins and fiber.

Buckwheat Flour: Buckwheat, contrary to its name, is not from the wheat family but from the rhubarb family, and it is gluten free. It is full of flavor and great for making pancakes, breads, and crêpes. It is high in niacin, iron, and fiber.

Chestnut Flour: Made from ground chestnuts, it has a distinctive rich flavor and is often used to make stuffing, pasta, breads, cookies, cakes, and other baked goods. Chestnut flour is high in vitamin C, fiber, and iron.

Coconut Flour: A soft flour made from dried coconut, it adds a sweet, light coconut taste when baking and is great for making breads, pancakes, cakes, and cookies. It is high in protein, fiber, fat, and manganese.

Corn Flour: Corn flour is often used in corn bread, tortillas, and muffins. It is high in fiber.

Cornmeal: Ground dried corn used to make cornbread, tamales, and polenta and as a coating for fried foods. Precooked cornmeal is also available, such as masa harina, which is great for making arepas and corn empanadas. Cornmeal is high in fiber.

Cornstarch: A starch made from corn, often used as a thickener in puddings, sauces, and baking.

Expandex: A modified food starch made from tapioca flour that can be used as a leavening agent in in breads and baked products to create a texture similar to gluten-containing baked foods.

Guar Gum: A powder made from a plant that works well as a leavening agent and to provide texture to baked products. It has a high fiber content, so you need to take care not to use too much in recipes because it can cause stomach problems for those who have sensitive stomachs and acts as a mild laxative.

Mesquite: Ground mesquite pods add cinnamon and chocolate flavors to food. Mesquite is high in fiber, protein, calcium, magnesium, potassium, iron, and zinc.

Millet Flour: Made from ground millet, it adds a sweet, nutty flavor. Millet flour is light in texture and high in folate, thiamine, niacin, and fiber.

Nut Flours: Nut flours are made from ground nuts. They work well in baked goods, providing better overall texture, and are especially flavorful in desserts. Most gluten-free flour blends will include almond, hazelnut, or chestnut flour. Since nuts are a common allergen, it is important to alert others when serving nut-based–flour foods. Nut flours are high in fiber and various nutrients, depending on which nut is used.

Potato Flour: Made from dried whole potatoes, this flour is heavy, with a strong potato taste. It works best added to gluten-free flour blends in small amounts. Too much potato flour can make baked goods dense and gummy. Potato flour is high in carbohydrates.

Potato Starch: Made from the dried starch component of peeled potatoes, this fine white powder is similar in texture to cornstarch. When added to gluten-free flour blends, it helps to lighten up baked products. It is also used as a thickener for gravies, sauces, custards, and puddings. It is high in carbohydrates.

Quinoa Flour: Quinoa is a high-protein grain loaded with nutrients. It adds a nutty flavor to baked goods and works well in pasta flour blends. Quinoa flour is high in protein and fiber.

Rice Flour: Rice flours are great when added to almost all flour blends, because they don't overpower the flavors in the recipe, and they have nice texture. Rice flours come in both fine and medium grinds; heavier grinds will require more liquid in recipes. It is high in carbohydrates.

Sorghum Flour: Sorghum takes on the flavor of other ingredients found in recipes and is ideal for putting together gluten-free flour blends. It is high in iron, selenium, fiber, and protein.

Soy Flour: This flour has a nutty taste and its higher protein content gives a nice texture to baked goods. It works well with other grains, especially when combined with stronger-flavored ingredients like chocolate, dried fruit, and nuts, and it is often found in gluten-free cookies and mixes. Soy has a short shelf life, so only buy it when you are going to use it. Some people with celiac disease are sensitive to soy proteins. Often, the soy found in baked goods is soy lecithin, or the fat component of the soy, which does not usually include the soy protein. Soy flour is high in protein and fiber.

Sweet Rice Flour: Sweet rice (also known as sticky or glutinous rice) does not contain gluten. It works well in sauces and tempura batter recipes. It is soft and fine and doesn't have that gritty texture that other rice flours sometimes have. Make sure you check mixes that include glutinous rice to make sure that other gluten-containing ingredients are not added. It is high in carbohydrates.

Tapioca Flour (also known as Tapioca Starch): Tapioca flour is made from the root of the cassava plant. It is often used in flour blends for baked goods as it gives bread a crisp, golden crust, adds a chewy texture to cookies, and generally lightens up otherwise heavy gluten-free baked goods. It is high in carbohydrates.

Teff Flour: Teff is a tiny grain that is high in iron and that is available as both a light and dark grain. It is great in flour blends and gives an earthy, hearty texture to baked goods. Teff flour is high in iron, thiamine, calcium, and fiber.

Xanthan Gum: A product that has been produced by the fermenting of corn sugar. Xanthan gum can be used as a thickener or as a leavening agent to produce a texture similar to that which gluten gives to bread recipes.

It is important to buy gluten-free grains and flours from a safe, uncontaminated source. Don't buy gluten-free flours or grains from places such as a health food store where they use the same scale to measure out their flours or grains—this could lead to contamination.

Baking with Gluten-Free Flour Blends

Baking with gluten-free flour blends takes patience and experimentation. You'll find that you'll get different results with different blends, and while you may like one blend for brownies, it may be a no-go for oatmeal raisin cookies or pizza crust. Don't despair! You've come to the right place for foolproof flour blends. With all the recipes in this book, you'll be making delicious breads, biscuits, cookies, and cakes in no time.

When you are ready to try adapting some of your own recipes, start by using a premixed, gluten-free blend. Brands I like include Bob's Red Mill, Pamela's Products, and King Arthur. Most gluten-free flour blends contain a combination of different flours and starches and some may even already have gums added to them. Popular combinations could include the following ingredients:

- 30% of a high-protein flour such as quinoa, soy, sorghum, almond, or bean flour

- 30% millet, rice, or coconut flour

- 40% tapioca flour or potato starch

When you start to feel more adventurous, try adding small amounts of different flours and starches to the premixed blends to tailor the flavor and texture to your preferences. Adding whole grain flours such as quinoa, sorghum, or millet to a gluten-free flour blend will also bump up its nutritional content. Most gluten-free flours are not fortified the same way that wheat flours are mandated to be in the United States. Eventually, you may feel comfortable enough to create your own unique flour blends and the premade percentages mentioned earlier can be a useful guide. Here are some of my gluten-free all-purpose flour blends:

Blend # 1

Great for breads and biscuits

Yields 4 cups

1½ cups tapioca flour

1 cup sorghum flour

½ cup coconut flour

½ cup potato starch

½ cup bean or nut flour

Blend # 2

Use to replace all-purpose flour, cup for cup, when coating meats and making breads, pizza, and other savory dishes.

Yields 4¾ cups

2 cups potato starch

1 cup sorghum or millet flour

¾ cup bean, soy, or nut flour

½ cup brown rice flour

½ cup tapioca flour

Blend # 3

Great for pancakes, waffles, baked goods, and desserts

Yields 5 cups

3 cups store-bought, gluten-free all-purpose flour blend

1 cup buckwheat flour

1 cup almond flour

For raised baked goods or foods that need better texture, such as pasta, I usually add 1 teaspoon of xanthan, guar gum, or expandex for each 1 to 3 cups of gluten-free flour blend. For example, for a baked good with a light crumb, I would add 1 teaspoon to 1 cup of gluten-free flour blend. For pasta, I would add 1 teaspoon to 2 cups of flour blend. For cake, I would add 1 teaspoon to 3 cups of flour blend. Adding ingredients such as cheese or other dairy products, fruit purees, nut butters, gelatins, vinegar, baking powder or baking soda, whipped egg whites, or seltzer also help provide better texture and crumb-feel to your final product.

Discovering the perfect flour blend for a recipe brings a tremendous sense of satisfaction, but if the thought of all of this experimenting gives you a headache and you just want a cookie already, turn to my chapters on Breads and Biscuits and Sweets and Treats for some foolproof favorites.

Preventing Cross-Contamination

One of the biggest challenges to following a 100% gluten-free diet is preventing the accidental cross-contamination of gluten-free products with gluten-containing products. I keep these dos and don'ts handy as an easy reminder of what to watch out for.

Dos

- Do buy condiments in squeeze bottles or buy separate spreadable products and mark them as gluten free.
- Do use clean and separate spatulas and utensils for cooking and serving gluten-free foods when gluten-containing foods are being cooked nearby.
- Do have a dedicated gluten-free toaster and colander.
- Do wipe down cooking surfaces before preparing foods.
- Do safely mark and separate all gluten-free products.
- Do cover surfaces that may be contaminated with gluten (such as putting aluminum foil or wax paper on a cookie sheet).

Don'ts

- Don't use a toaster or colander that has been used with gluten-containing foods.
- Don't use wooden spoons or wood cutting boards.
- Don't use a shared fryer to fry gluten-free foods. Heat doesn't "kill" the gluten.
- Don't cook gluten-free pasta in the same water as regular pasta.

Avoid these common contamination mistakes:

Putting gluten-containing meatballs into the tomato sauce.

Placing a utensil that has been used to spread dip, butter, margarine, jam, peanut butter, or mayonnaise on a gluten-containing piece of bread or cracker back in the container. Make sure you mark spreads "gluten free" or "gluten containing" so there are no mistakes, or buy squeeze bottles whenever possible. Similarly, dipping a gluten-containing cracker into a gluten-free dip or spread. Separate foods to avoid this issue.

Cooking gluten-free foods uncovered in the oven below gluten-containing food: it's too easy for crumbs from the gluten-containing food to contaminate the food below. Always cook gluten-free choices on the highest oven rack so nothing with gluten falls into the food.

The Gluten-Free, Hassle-Free Cookbook

Breakfast

Before I was gluten free, we ate fresh bagels for breakfast on Sundays and I loved going out for brunch on holidays and special occasions. I would stroll through the buffet adding waffles, omelets, and muffins to my plate, without thinking about their ingredients. Now when I go out for breakfast I usually have eggs—after convincing the chef to prepare them in a separate pan, away from the pancakes. There are some hotels and restaurants that do cater to those who are gluten free; however, the selections are usually no match for those memorable buffets.

I created these delicious, gluten-free breakfast foods so you will never feel disappointed again. Make every morning a special occasion with sausage and cheese biscuits, baked blueberry coconut oatmeal crisps, cheese blintzes, buckwheat pancakes with cinnamon apples, pumpkin raisin muffins with pecan streusel, and more. And since we're all so busy, I've made sure many of these recipes, such as my breakfast cookies, can be eaten on the go or made ahead on the weekend for quick and healthy breakfasts during the week.

Baked Blueberry Coconut Oatmeal Crisp

Whole Grain Breakfast Cookies

Sausage and Cheese Biscuits

Parmesan Herb Egg Soufflé

Cheese Blintzes with Fresh Strawberries and Whipped Cream

Buckwheat Pancakes with Cinnamon Apples

Pumpkin Raisin Muffins with Pecan Streusel

Aunt Ann's Famous Baked French Toast

Creamy Yogurt Shake

Cranberry Almond Scones

 *Quick and easy*

Baked Blueberry Coconut Oatmeal Crisp

SERVES 8

GF, MF, EF, SF, NF, PF, FF, SFF, V, VG

Tired of a traditional bowl of oatmeal? Try this cake-like breakfast bar without losing any of the nutritional punch. Perfect.

2 cups light coconut milk

1½ cups gluten-free oats

¼ cup packed brown sugar

½ cup gluten-free sweetened shredded coconut

½ cup ground flaxseed

2 teaspoons pure vanilla extract

1 cup fresh or frozen blueberries (if using frozen, defrost and drain them first)

1. Preheat oven to 350 degrees F. Line a 9-inch square baking pan with parchment paper.

2. Mix all ingredients together in a large bowl. Press into baking pan and bake for 40 to 50 minutes, until firm. Cut into eight bars and serve.

Nutritional information: 251 calories, 7.5 grams of protein, 32.8 grams of carbohydrates, 10 grams of fat, 0 milligrams of cholesterol, 28.6 milligrams of sodium, 5.8 grams of fiber, 41.6 milligrams of calcium, 2.2 milligrams of iron

FODMAPs

- To make FODMAP friendly, substitute chia seeds for the flax and brown sugar for the white sugar.

TIPS: Prepare ingredients on baking sheet the night before, refrigerate, and bake in the morning. Bars keep well for several days stored in a cookie tin or wrapped in aluminum foil.

Whole Grain Breakfast Cookies   SERVES 12

GF, PF*, FF, SFF, V

An easy grab-and-go breakfast to start your day! Combining walnuts, oatmeal, dried fruit, and hemp hearts (shelled hemp seeds) packs a nutritional punch. High in fiber, these cookies will keep you full until lunch.

½ cup brown rice flour

½ cup tapioca flour

¼ cup almond flour

½ teaspoon baking soda

1 teaspoon ground cinnamon

½ teaspoon sea salt

2 tablespoons unsalted butter, softened

⅓ cup brown sugar

1 egg

2 medium bananas, mashed

1 teaspoon pure vanilla extract

½ cup gluten-free oatmeal

½ cup gluten-free granola

¼ cup raw shelled sunflower seeds

¼ cup chopped walnuts

¼ cup dried cranberries

2 tablespoons hemp hearts

1. Preheat oven to 350 degrees F. Line a baking sheet with parchment paper.

2. Whisk together flours, baking soda, cinnamon, and salt in a medium size bowl.

3. In a large bowl, beat butter and brown sugar together with an electric mixer until well combined. Beat in egg, bananas, and vanilla until well mixed.

4. Add flour mixture and beat until well combined.

5. Stir in oatmeal, granola, sunflower seeds, walnuts, cranberries, and hemp hearts.

6. Drop by 2-tablespoon scoops onto prepared cookie sheet. Flatten slightly. Bake for 12 to 15 minutes, or until cookies are light brown on top but still soft.

7. Transfer to a cooling rack to cool completely.

Nutritional information: 186 calories, 3.9 grams of protein, 26 grams of carbohydrates, 7.9 grams of fat, 20.5 milligrams of cholesterol, 153.4 milligrams of sodium, 2.4 grams of fiber, 21.2 milligrams of calcium, 1.5 milligrams of iron

Allergen Notes and Additional Allergen Substitutions

- To keep peanut free, check the gluten-free granola for peanuts.
- To make milk free, substitute margarine for the butter and check the granola for milk.
- To make egg free, use a gluten-free, eggless egg substitute.
- To make soy free, use soy-free, gluten-free granola.
- To make vegan, substitute margarine or vegetable oil for the butter and use a gluten-free, vegan egg substitute.

TIP: These cookies freeze nicely. Freeze cookies on a baking sheet, wrap individually in plastic wrap, and store in a freezer bag. To serve, unwrap and defrost in the microwave for 20 seconds or in a 350 degree F oven for 10 minutes.

Sausage and Cheese Biscuits   SERVES 8

GF, EF, SF*, NF*, PF, FF, SFF

These biscuits make for a hearty breakfast or a satisfying lunch paired with eggs, a salad, or soup.

For the sausage:

1 tablespoon olive oil

1 shallot, finely chopped

½ pound lean ground breast of chicken

1 tablespoon fresh sage, finely chopped

½ teaspoon fennel seed, chopped

¼ teaspoon ground allspice

½ teaspoon salt

¼ teaspoon pepper

For the biscuits:

2 cups gluten-free all-purpose flour blend such as blend #2 (page xxiv)

1 tablespoon gluten-free baking powder

1 teaspoon baking soda

½ teaspoon salt

½ teaspoon xanthan gum

8 tablespoons (1 stick) cold unsalted butter

½ cup shredded, reduced-fat sharp cheddar cheese

1 cup buttermilk (or 1 cup whole milk mixed with 1 tablespoon white vinegar)

¼ cup white rice flour

1. *To make the sausage:* Heat oil in a medium nonstick skillet over medium heat. Add shallot and sauté for 5 minutes, until softened and beginning to brown.

2. Add ground chicken, sage, fennel seed, allspice, salt, and pepper. Cook, stirring frequently, until meat is browned and cooked through. Remove from heat. Cool completely.

3. *To make the biscuits:* Heat oven to 400 degrees F. Line a baking sheet with parchment paper.

4. Sift together gluten-free flour, baking powder, baking soda, salt, and xanthan gum into a large bowl. Cut in butter until coarse crumbs are formed. Stir in chicken mixture and cheese.

5. Add the buttermilk. Gently stir the mixture until all dry ingredients are moistened. Work dough with your hands until it comes together.

6. Lightly coat work surface with white rice flour. Turn dough out and flatten to about ¾-inch thick. Cut with 2½-inch round biscuit cutter. Place on prepared baking sheet. Gather dough scraps together and press out to ¾-inch thick. Cut additional biscuits.

7. Bake for 15 to 16 minutes, until golden brown. Cool slightly before serving.

Nutritional information: 377 calories, 10.4 grams of protein, 45.7 grams of carbohydrates, 17.9 grams of fat, 57.8 milligrams of cholesterol, 602 milligrams of sodium, <1 gram of fiber, 313 milligrams of calcium, 1.2 milligrams of iron

Allergen Notes and Additional Allergen Substitutions

- To keep soy and nut free, check the gluten-free flour blend for soy and nuts.
- To make milk free, substitute vegetable shortening for the butter, substitute rice, coconut, or almond milk mixed with 1 tablespoon white vinegar for the buttermilk, and use a milk-free cheddar cheese.

FODMAPs

- To make FODMAP friendly, for the sausage, omit the fennel seeds and substitute 2 chopped green onions (green part only) for the shallots. For the biscuits, substitute lactose-free, rice, or coconut milk mixed with 1 tablespoon white vinegar for the buttermilk.

TIPS: This recipe also works well with ground turkey. For the best biscuits use frozen butter and grate into sifted flour. Store dough in the freezer until ready to make biscuits. You can also make these biscuits ahead of time and freeze them. To serve, microwave for one minute.

Parmesan Herb Egg Soufflé SERVES 4

GF, NF, PF, FF, SFF, V

This light, airy soufflé is easy to make and sure to impress. It must be served right away though, so have everyone ready at the table when it comes out of the oven. Use fresh herbs for a truly memorable breakfast choice.

1 tablespoon olive oil

¼ cup white rice flour

¼ teaspoon sea salt

¼ teaspoon black pepper

1 cup 1% milk

½ cup plus 2 tablespoons grated Parmesan cheese

4 egg whites at room temperature

½ teaspoon cream of tartar

4 egg yolks

1 tablespoon chopped fresh parsley

1 tablespoon chopped fresh basil

1 tablespoon chopped fresh thyme

Gluten-free cooking spray

1. Preheat oven to 375 degrees F.

2. Heat oil in a medium saucepan over medium-high heat. Stir in flour, salt, and pepper. Cook for one minute.

3. Gradually whisk in milk and cook, stirring constantly, until the sauce boils and starts to thicken. Remove from heat and stir in ½ cup of cheese.

4. Beat the egg yolks into the cheese sauce one at a time until well blended. Stir in parsley, basil, and thyme.

5. In a clean bowl, beat egg whites and cream of tartar until stiff (but not dry) peaks form.

6. Gently but thoroughly fold egg whites into egg yolk mixture until no streaks of white remain.

7. Spray four 8-ounce ramekins with cooking spray, coat with remaining Parmesan, then tap out the excess. Gently pour egg mixture into the ramekins. Bake until puffed and brown, about 20 minutes. Serve immediately.

Nutrition information: 219 calories, 13.8 grams of protein, 12.3 grams of carbohydrates, 12.4 grams of fat, 200 milligrams of cholesterol, 427 milligrams of sodium, <1 gram of fiber, 249.7 milligrams of calcium, 1.2 milligrams of iron

Allergen Notes and Additional Allergen Substitutions

- To make milk free, use dairy-free milk and cheese.
- To make soy free, use soy-free cooking spray.

FODMAPs

- To make FODMAP friendly, use lactose-free milk.

TIP: It's easier to separate eggs cleanly when they are cold; however, egg whites whip to a greater volume when they are at room temperature.

Cheese Blintzes with Fresh Strawberries and Whipped Cream   SERVES 6

GF, NF, PF, FF, SFF, V

Filled with sweet, creamy cheese, these blintzes make a spectacular beginning to any day.

For the crepes:

⅔ cup sorghum flour

⅓ cup tapioca flour

1 tablespoon powdered sugar

2 eggs

1 cup low-fat milk

½ teaspoon sea salt

2 tablespoons salted butter, melted

Gluten-free cooking spray

For the filling:

1 cup part-skim ricotta cheese

1 (8-ounce) package light cream cheese

¼ cup granulated sugar

2 teaspoons lemon juice

1 teaspoon pure vanilla extract

Garnish

2 cups fresh strawberries, sliced

whipped cream, to taste

1. *To make the crepes:* Place flours, powdered sugar, eggs, milk, salt, and melted butter in a blender. Blend until smooth.

2. Spray an 8-inch skillet with cooking spray and heat over medium heat.

3. Place about 3 tablespoons of crepe batter onto skillet. Tilt the pan with a circular motion so the batter coats the surface evenly. Cook for about one minute, until the crepe begins to bubble and dry. Flip over and cook for another 15 seconds.

Crepes should be pliable and lightly brown. Keep crepes warm under a towel while you use up the rest of the batter. Yield should be 12 crepes.

4. *To make the filling:* With an electric mixer, beat the ricotta cheese, cream cheese, sugar, lemon juice, and vanilla extract until smooth.

5. *To assemble:* Preheat oven to 300 degrees F. Line a baking sheet with parchment paper.

6. Place 2 tablespoons of cheese filling in each crepe. Roll up and place on baking sheet. Bake in the oven for 10 minutes, or until crepes are warmed through. Some cheese may ooze out of the ends. Serve topped with strawberries and whipped cream.

Nutritional information: 339 calories, 11.9 grams of protein, 35.3 grams of carbohydrates, 15.7 grams of fat, 111.3 milligrams of cholesterol, 437.9 milligrams of sodium, 1.8 grams of fiber, 231.5 milligrams of calcium, 1 milligram of iron

Allergen Notes and Additional Allergen Substitutions

- To make egg free, use a gluten-free, eggless egg substitute.
- To make soy free, use soy-free cooking spray.

TIPS: These blintzes can be warmed in a skillet instead of the oven. Add a small amount of butter to a skillet over medium heat and cook blintzes for one minute per side, until golden. If blintz doesn't feel warm enough, cover the pan and heat for one to two minutes more. Top with your favorite fruit.

Buckwheat Pancakes with Cinnamon Apples   SERVES 6

GF, EF, SF*, NF, PF, FF, SFF, V

Buckwheat adds an earthy color and a nutritional punch to this fluffy pancake.

For the cinnamon apple topping:

3 small apples (such as Macintosh)

1 teaspoon pure vanilla extract

1 teaspoon ground cinnamon

¼ teaspoon ground nutmeg

1 tablespoon unsalted butter

For the pancakes:

¾ cup buckwheat flour

¼ cup oat flour

½ cup white rice flour

3 tablespoons granulated sugar

½ teaspoon ground cinnamon

½ teaspoon sea salt

1 teaspoon baking soda

½ cup unsweetened applesauce

1 cup low-fat milk

Gluten-free cooking spray or 1 teaspoon olive oil

1. *To make the topping:* Peel, core, and cut apples into ½-inch-thick slices. Mix with vanilla, cinnamon, and nutmeg.

2. Melt butter in a medium skillet over medium heat. Add apples and cook, stirring occasionally, until apples are tender and browned. Remove from heat and set aside.

3. *To make the pancakes:* In a large bowl, whisk together flours, sugar, cinnamon, salt, and baking soda. Stir in applesauce and milk until combined.

4. Heat a griddle or nonstick frying pan over medium heat. Spray with cooking spray. Using a ¼-cup measure, pour batter onto the hot surface. Cook for two to three minutes on one side, then flip over and cook one to two minutes more, or until nicely browned.

5. Serve topped with warm apples.

Nutritional information: 216 calories, 5 grams of protein, 41.7 grams of carbohydrates, 4.3 grams of fat, 71 milligrams of cholesterol, 423 milligrams of sodium, 4.6 grams of fiber, 64 milligrams of calcium, 1 milligram of iron

Allergen Notes and Additional Allergen Substitutions

- To keep soy free, use a soy-free cooking spray or olive oil.
- To make milk free, substitute margarine for the butter and use dairy-free milk.
- To make vegan, substitute coconut oil for the butter and use dairy-free milk.

TIP: Keep pancakes warm in a 250 degree F oven until all are cooked and ready to serve.

 *Quick and easy*

Pumpkin Raisin Muffins with Pecan Streusel   SERVES 12

GF, PF, FF, SFF, V

These moist muffins are bursting with pumpkin flavor!

For the muffins:

1½ cups gluten-free all-purpose flour blend

½ cup gluten-free oats

1 teaspoon baking soda

½ teaspoon gluten-free baking powder

½ teaspoon sea salt

1 teaspoon ground cinnamon

½ teaspoon ground nutmeg

½ teaspoon ground ginger

¼ teaspoon ground cloves

1 cup pumpkin puree

¼ cup granulated sugar

¼ cup brown sugar

¼ cup vegetable oil

2 eggs

1 teaspoon pure vanilla extract

¼ cup buttermilk (or ¼ cup whole milk mixed with ¼ tablespoon white vinegar)

½ cup raisins

For the streusel:

1 tablespoon unsalted butter

2 tablespoons brown sugar

2 tablespoons gluten-free oats

1 tablespoon tapioca flour

2 tablespoons chopped pecans

1. Preheat oven to 375 degrees F. Line 12 muffin cups with paper liners.

2. *To make muffins:* In a large bowl, whisk together flour, oats, baking soda, baking powder, salt, cinnamon, nutmeg, ginger, cloves, sugar, and brown sugar.

3. In a separate bowl, mix together oil, eggs, vanilla, and buttermilk. Add wet ingredients to flour mixture and stir until just combined. Stir in raisins.

4. Scoop batter into prepared muffin cups, filling to top.

5. *To make streusel:* In a small bowl, combine brown sugar, oats, tapioca flour, and pecans. Add butter and incorporate well using a pastry blender or two knives. Mixture will be crumbly. Sprinkle on top of muffins.

6. Bake for 20 minutes, or until toothpick inserted into muffin comes out clean.

Nutritional information: 230.8 calories, 3.2 grams of protein, 37.8 grams of carbohydrates, 7.5 grams of fat, 33.7 milligrams of cholesterol, 221.2 milligrams of sodium, 1.7 grams of fiber, 50.8 milligrams of calcium, 1.1 milligrams of iron

Allergen Notes and Additional Allergen Substitutions

- To make milk free, substitute rice, coconut, or almond milk mixed with ¼ tablespoon white vinegar for the buttermilk and margarine for the butter.

- To make egg free, use a gluten-free, eggless egg substitute.

- To make soy free, use soy-free oil.

- To make nut free, omit the pecans.

TIP: Replace raisins with dried cranberries or dried apples.

Aunt Ann's Famous Baked French Toast   SERVES 8

GF, NF, PF, FF, SFF, V

My Aunt Ann always serves the most amazing New Year's brunch with this baked French toast as a featured favorite.

> 6 tablespoons salted butter
>
> ¾ cup packed brown sugar
>
> 1 tablespoon corn syrup
>
> Gluten-free cooking spray
>
> 8 slices gluten-free bread (such as Udis)
>
> 4 eggs
>
> 1 cup 2% milk
>
> 1 teaspoon pure vanilla extract
>
> 2 teaspoons ground cinnamon
>
> 2 tablespoons powdered sugar

1. Melt butter. Add brown sugar and corn syrup and combine well.

2. Spray a 9 × 13-inch pan with cooking spray. Pour butter mixture into baking dish and arrange bread slices flat in butter mixture. Squeeze to fit in.

3. Use a blender to mix eggs, milk, and vanilla. Pour over bread slices, covering completely. Sprinkle cinnamon on top of bread slices.

4. Cover and refrigerate overnight.

5. Uncover and bake at 350 degrees F for 30 minutes. Dust with powdered sugar.

Nutritional information: 176.9 calories, 3.1 grams of protein, 20.7 grams of carbohydrates, 8.7 grams of fat, 78.8 milligrams of cholesterol, 169.2 milligrams of sodium, 1.5 grams of fiber, 47 milligrams of calcium, <1 milligram of iron

Allergen Notes and Additional Allergen Substitutions

- To make milk free, substitute margarine for the butter and use dairy-free milk.
- To make egg free, use a gluten-free, eggless egg substitute and egg-free bread.

- To make soy free, use soy-free cooking spray and soy-free bread.
- To make vegan, substitute margarine for the butter and use vegan, gluten-free bread, dairy-free milk, and a gluten-free, vegan egg substitute.

TIP: Experiment with different types of bread. If you're feeling decadent, try using large pieces of gluten-free muffins or slices of pound cake in place of the gluten-free bread.

 *Quick and easy*

Creamy Yogurt Shake   SERVES 2

GF, EF, NF, PF, FF, SFF, V

Flaxseeds add fiber and omega-3 fatty acids to this refreshing shake. Change it up with chia seeds. A dollop of whipped topping adds a little decadence.

- 1 cup gluten-free, low-fat vanilla Greek yogurt
- 1 cup non-fat milk
- 1 frozen peeled banana cut into 2-inch pieces
- 1½ cups of hulled strawberries
- ½ teaspoon pure vanilla extract
- 1 teaspoon ground cinnamon
- 2 tablespoons ground flaxseed
- 2 tablespoons fat-free, gluten-free whipped topping (such as Cool Whip)

1. Place all ingredients except whipped topping in a blender and blend until creamy. Serve with a dollop of whipped topping.

Nutritional information: 264.5 calories, 17.7 grams of protein, 41 grams of carbohydrates, 4.1 grams of fat, 2.4 milligrams of cholesterol, 103 milligrams of sodium, 6.3 grams of fiber, 334.6 milligrams of calcium, 1 milligram of iron

Allergen Notes and Additional Allergen Substitutions

- To make milk free and vegan, use a dairy-free yogurt and milk.
- To make soy free, use a soy-free whipped topping or omit.

FODMAPs

- To make FODMAP friendly, use lactose-free milk and yogurt, and omit the flax seed and whipped topping.

TIPS: Any flavor of gluten-free yogurt, such as coconut or cherry, works great in this recipe. If you're pressed for time, prepare the night before, keep refrigerated, and give it a shake the next morning before serving.

Cranberry Almond Scones SERVES 8

GF, SF, PF, FF, SFF, V

Almond meal adds just the right texture to these scones. Serve warm with your favorite jam.

½ cup sorghum flour

¾ cup white rice flour

½ cup tapioca flour

¼ cup almond flour

¼ cup granulated sugar

1 tablespoon gluten-free baking powder

½ teaspoon sea salt

½ cup (8 tablespoons) cold unsalted butter

¼ cup dried cranberries

1 teaspoon orange zest

2 tablespoons slivered almonds

1 egg

¾ cup half-and-half

1. Preheat oven to 450 degrees F. Line a baking sheet with parchment paper.

2. In a large bowl, whisk together flours, sugar, baking powder, and salt. Cut in butter with a pastry blender or two knives until mixture is crumbly.

3. Add cranberries, orange zest, and almonds to flour mixture.

4. In a separate bowl, whisk together egg and half-and-half. Stir into flour mixture until just combined.

5. Place dough between two sheets of waxed paper. Pat out into a 7-inch circle, then cut into eight wedges or use a biscuit cutter to cut into 2-inch rounds. Place on prepared baking sheet.

6. Bake for 13 to 15 minutes, until golden.

Nutritional information: 332 calories, 4.5 grams of protein, 38.4 grams of carbohydrates, 18.7 grams of fat, 62.1 milligrams of cholesterol, 157.9 milligrams of sodium, 2.1 grams of fiber, 276.2 milligrams of calcium, <1 milligram of iron

Allergen Notes and Additional Allergen Substitutions

- To make milk free, substitute margarine for the butter and rice milk for the half-and-half.

- To make egg free, use a gluten-free, eggless egg substitute.

- To make nut free, substitute ¼ cup sorghum flour for the almond meal and omit the almonds.

- To make vegan, substitute margarine or ½ cup of corn oil for the butter, substitute rice milk for the half-and-half, and use a gluten-free, vegan egg substitute.

FODMAPs

- To make FODMAP friendly, substitute walnut flour for the almond flour, substitute chopped walnuts for the slivered almonds, and omit the cranberries.

TIP: Scones are very versatile. You can make them plain or add your favorite combinations of fruit and nuts. If you want to glaze them, mix ½ cup powdered sugar with 1 to 2 tablespoons half-and-half and drizzle on top.

Starters

I have often heard people say that the hors d'oeuvres are their favorite part of a meal, so whenever I entertain I try to serve a variety of delectable selections. This collection of starters are perfect for passing-around during a cocktail party or being served on a platter during a sit down meal. I have selected these recipes particularly because they are rarely available gluten free, especially the sliders, pigs in a blanket, crab cakes, dumplings, and spring rolls.

Arepa Sliders

Crab Cakes

Pork Dumplings

Spring Rolls with Peanut Dipping Sauce

Bruschetta

Cheese Puffs, Mini Knishes, and Pigs in a Blanket

Crunchy Baked Chicken Tenders with Honey Mustard
   Dipping Sauce

Potato Pierogies

Crispy Zucchini Sticks

Cheesy Polenta Toasts with Roasted Mushrooms and Spinach

Batter-Fried Onion Rings

 *Quick and easy*

Arepa Sliders SERVES 8

GF, EF, SF, NF, PF, FF, SFF

Arepas are easy to make and so versatile. I like to fill these flat corn cakes with salami and provolone cheese, but you can fill yours with anything you like: meat (perfect for mini burgers, grilled chicken. or pulled pork), eggs, veggies, even salad. These sliders are always a hit.

> 1 cup precooked, dried, gluten-free cornmeal (often available in the Spanish foods section of the grocery store)
>
> 1 cup hot water
>
> 1 teaspoon sea salt
>
> 2 tablespoons granulated sugar
>
> ⅛ pound provolone cheese, sliced thin
>
> ⅛ pound Genoa salami, sliced thin
>
> 2 tablespoons olive oil

1. Mix together all ingredients except the provolone and salami. Work dough into a ball and let it rest for five minutes.

2. Shape dough into eight golf-ball size balls and flatten slightly.

3. In a large nonstick skillet, heat oil over medium-high heat until it shimmers. Fry arepas on each side until golden brown. Remove from oil and drain on paper towels.

4. Carefully cut arepas open and place one slice of cheese and meat in each slider.

5. Bake in a 350 degree F oven until cheese melts.

Nutritional information: 154.4 calories, 4.5 grams of protein, 17.1 grams of carbohydrates, 7.4 grams of fat, 11.1 milligrams of cholesterol, 453.5 milligrams of sodium, <1 gram of fiber, 54.7 milligrams of calcium, <1 milligram of iron

Allergen Notes and Additional Allergen Substitutions

- To make milk free, omit the cheese or use a milk-free cheese.
- To make vegetarian, omit the salami.
- To make vegan, substitute grilled veggies for the cheese and salami.

FODMAP Friendly

TIP: Premade unsliced arepas can be kept wrapped in plastic in the refrigerator for up to a week. To serve, heat in a warm oven to soften, slice, and fill.

 *Quick and easy*

Crab Cakes SERVES 6

GF, NF, PF, FF

So crispy and delicious everyone will want one! I love crab cakes and was determined to create a perfect gluten-free version. The potato chips add extra flavor and are less expensive and more readily available than gluten-free bread crumbs. If you've been missing crab cakes, you will flip for this recipe.

½ cup crushed gluten-free potato chips

12 ounces lump crabmeat, picked over

1 tablespoon dried minced onion

1 egg

2 tablespoons gluten-free, low-fat blue cheese salad dressing or mayonnaise

1½ teaspoons yellow mustard

¼ teaspoon sea salt

¼ teaspoon black pepper

2 tablespoons lemon juice

1 teaspoon dried paprika

Dash Old Bay seasoning

⅓ cup potato starch or tapioca flour

¼ cup corn oil

1. Combine all ingredients except potato starch or tapioca flour and corn oil until well combined.

2. Form into six 1-inch-thick patties. (If too wet to hold together, add more crushed potato chips.)

3. Dredge crab cakes in tapioca or potato starch, coating both sides well.

4. Heat corn oil in a large skillet over high heat until oil shimmers. Lower heat to medium.

5. Fry crab cakes until golden brown on both sides.

Nutritional information: 207.8 calories, 9.9 grams of protein, 10.9 grams of carbohydrates, 14.1 grams of fat, 81.8 milligrams of cholesterol, 498 milligrams of sodium, <1 gram of fiber, 29.3 milligrams of calcium, <1 milligram of iron

Allergen Notes and Additional Allergen Substitutions

- To make egg free, use a gluten-free eggless egg substitute and an eggless mayonnaise.
- To make milk free, use mayonnaise to replace the blue cheese dressing.
- To make soy free, use soy-free potato chips and mayonnaise.

FODMAPs

- To make FODMAP friendly, substitute chopped green onion for the dried minced onion, and use mayonnaise.

TIPS: Do not substitute imitation crabmeat, as it may contain gluten. Serve on a bed of shredded lettuce and cabbage, with sliced tomato, sliced onion, lemon wedges, and gluten-free tartar or cocktail sauce. These crab cakes are great served rolled in a warm corn tortilla. Freeze cooked crab cakes on a baking sheet, wrap individually in plastic wrap, and store in a freezer bag. When you have a craving, defrost in the refrigerator, unwrap, and bake in the oven until warmed through.

Pork Dumplings   SERVES 24

GF, MF, EF, NF, PF, FF, SFF

A favorite often missed by those following a gluten-free diet. Most restaurants use egg roll wrappers that are made from wheat mixed with rice to make their dumplings. My version uses rice paper alone. Sometimes I fill these wrappers with veggies or use ground chicken, turkey, or shrimp instead of the pork.

For dumplings:

- 1 pound lean ground pork lean
- 3 tablespoons gluten-free soy sauce
- 1 (10-ounce) package frozen chopped spinach, defrosted and squeezed dry
- 1 teaspoon sugar
- 1 tablespoon minced fresh ginger
- 1 tablespoon white wine
- 1 tablespoon cornstarch
- 2 green onions, finely chopped, plus more for garnish
- 2 tablespoons sesame oil, divided
- 16 (8.5-inch) 100% rice paper spring roll wrappers, each round wrapper cut into thirds
- Gluten-free all-purpose flour blend, for dusting

For dipping sauce:

- ¼ cup gluten-free light soy sauce
- 2 tablespoons white vinegar
- 1 tablespoon minced ginger
- Hot sauce to taste
- 2 teaspoons sugar
- 1 teaspoon sesame oil

1. *To make the dumplings:* Mix together all ingredients except the rice paper and half the sesame oil.
2. Dip rice paper into warm water until soft, remove, and shake off excess water.

3. Place a dumpling wrapper on a lightly floured work surface and spoon about ½ tablespoon of the filling in the middle. Wrap paper loosely around filling by folding in the corners and gently rolling closed. Since the rice paper is damp it will seal shut. Repeat with remaining dumpling wrappers and filling. Place on a baking sheet that has been covered with waxed paper and freeze for 15 minutes. If you want the dumplings to hold together even tighter, freeze for 30 minutes.

4. Drizzle remaining sesame oil on a plate and arrange partially frozen dumplings on the plate. Place the plate in a bamboo steamer over a pot of simmering water. If it is a small steamer or if all the dumplings don't fit on one plate, you may need to do several batches or place in multiple layers of the steamer.

5. Steam for 10 minutes until cooked through.

6. *To make dipping sauce:* Mix all ingredients together, and refrigerate until ready to serve.

7. To serve, garnish steamed dumplings with additional green onions; dipping sauce can be drizzled over the dumplings or served alongside.

Nutritional information, dumplings: 70 calories, 3.5 grams of protein, 7.3 grams of carbohydrates, 2.8 grams of fat, 9.1 milligrams of cholesterol, 160 milligrams of sodium, <1 gram of fiber, 11.7 milligrams of calcium, <1 milligram of iron

Nutritional information, dipping sauce: 5.5 calories, <1 gram of protein, .7 grams of carbohydrates, <1 gram of fat, 0 milligrams of cholesterol, 94 milligrams of sodium, <1 gram of fiber, <1 milligram of calcium, <1 milligram of iron

Allergen Notes and Additional Allergen Substitutions

- To make vegetarian and vegan, substitute finely chopped mixed vegetables for the pork.

FODMAPs

- To make dumplings FODMAP friendly, only use the green part of the onions and add one additional chopped green onion. Dipping sauce is FODMAP friendly.

> **TIP:** Make dumplings ahead, freeze on a baking sheet, and store in a freezer bag until ready to cook. Try chicken, ground turkey, or finely chopped mixed vegetables instead of pork. Use this versatile dipping sauce alongside spring rolls and wontons or over rice noodles.

 *Quick and easy*

Spring Rolls with Peanut Dipping Sauce   SERVES 8

GF, MF, EF, NF, FF, SFF, V, VG

Filled with vegetables, these rolls pack lots of flavor into a small package. I love spring rolls but it is almost impossible to find them gluten free. These are so flavorful and crispy that you will love every bite.

For spring rolls:

1 (3.75-ounce) package bean threads (available in Asian markets and in international aisles in the supermarket)

2 cups finely sliced green cabbage

½ cup chopped green onions

1 cup chopped fresh spinach

½ finely diced cucumber

½ cup shredded carrots

½ cup chopped fresh parsley

2 tablespoons gluten-free soy sauce

2 tablespoons lime juice

1 teaspoon fresh grated ginger

½ teaspoon red pepper flakes

16 (8.5-inch) rice paper spring roll wrappers

¼ cup olive oil

For peanut dipping sauce:

4 tablespoons gluten-free soy sauce

2 tablespoons creamy peanut butter

1 tablespoon maple syrup

2 teaspoons white wine vinegar

¼ teaspoon garlic powder

2 teaspoons sesame oil

1 teaspoon red pepper flakes

1. Soak bean threads in warm water for four to five minutes, until softened. Drain.

2. Toss together bean threads, cabbage, green onion, cucumber, carrots, and parsley in a large bowl.

3. In a small bowl, mix soy sauce, lime juice, ginger, and red pepper flakes. Add to cabbage mixture and mix well.

4. Submerge spring roll wrappers in hot water until pliable, about 15 seconds. Remove from water and shake off excess. Place 2 tablespoons of filling in each wrapper. Fold in sides and roll up tightly.

5. Heat olive oil in a large frying pan over medium high heat. In batches, fry spring rolls until browned. Make sure the rice paper is dry before frying. Remove from oil and drain on paper towels.

6. *To make peanut dipping sauce:* Whisk all ingredients together in a small bowl. Serve with spring rolls.

Nutrition information, spring rolls: 247.8 calories, 3.5 grams of protein, 36 grams of carbohydrates, 10 grams of fat, 0 milligrams of cholesterol, 477 milligrams of sodium, 2.2 grams of fiber, 32.7 milligrams of calcium, 1.2 milligrams of iron

Nutrition information, peanut dipping sauce: 46.6 calories, 1.4 grams of protein, 3 grams of carbohydrates, 3.2 grams of fat, 0 milligrams of cholesterol, 306.7 milligrams of sodium, <1 gram of fiber, 3 milligrams of calcium, <1 milligram of iron

Allergen Notes and Additional Allergen Substitutions

- To make soy free, omit soy sauce and add a pinch of extra salt for the dumplings and omit the peanut dipping sauce. Gluten-free duck sauce can be used as a soy-free alternative for dipping (most duck sauce is naturally gluten free).

- To make peanut free, omit the peanut dipping sauce or omit the peanut butter and substitute sesame oil mixed with 2 tablespoons of sesame seed paste (tahini).

FODMAPs

- To make FODMAP friendly, omit the bean threads and substitute 2 teaspoons of garlic-infused oil (page 31) for garlic powder in the peanut dipping sauce.

TIP: Make spring rolls crispier by rolling in potato starch before frying.

 *Quick and easy*

A FODMAP-Friendly Staple

Garlic-Infused Oil SERVES 8

GF, MF, EF, SF, NF, PF, FF, SFF, V, VG

This rich, flavorful oil is simple to make and an excellent FODMAP-friendly substitute for fresh garlic or garlic powder in many recipes. Try it drizzled over roasted vegetables or mashed potatoes.

½ cup extra virgin olive oil

4 cloves garlic, peeled and washed, partially crushed

1. Place oil and garlic in a saucepan over a low heat. When the oil starts to bubble around the garlic for about five minutes, remove from heat and let cool.

2. Drain through a fine mesh strainer to remove garlic cloves.

3. Pour garlic oil into a clean jar with a lid.

4. Keep stored in the refrigerator for up to a week. It is important to keep the oil refrigerated because the garlic may cause harmful bacteria to grow if left at room temperature.

Nutritional information: 119 calories, 0 grams of protein, 0 grams of carbohydrates, 0 milligrams of fat, 0 milligrams of cholesterol, <1 milligram of sodium, <1 gram of fiber, <1 milligram of calcium, <1 milligram of iron.

 *Quick and easy*

Bruschetta   SERVES 12

GF, NF, PF, FF, SFF, V

Toasting the gluten-free bread first prevents the bread from getting soggy and the lime juice and capers really make this recipe pop. If they're available, use vine-ripened tomatoes.

1 loaf (6 ounces) gluten-free Italian bread (such as Everybody Eats, or use the recipe for homemade French bread on page 88)

Gluten-free cooking spray

1 teaspoon onion powder

1 teaspoon garlic powder

3 cups chopped tomato, seeded and liquid drained

1 small red onion, chopped fine

2 tablespoons chopped fresh basil

2 tablespoons olive oil

1 to 2 tablespoons chopped fresh garlic

1 lime, juiced

2 tablespoons capers

1 teaspoon sea salt

½ teaspoon pepper

1. Preheat oven to 400 degrees F.

2. Spray a baking sheet with cooking spray.

3. Slice Italian bread into ¼-inch-thick pieces and arrange on baking sheet.

4. Spray top of Italian bread with cooking spray and sprinkle with onion and garlic powder.

5. Bake until outside just starts to brown. Store in an airtight container until ready to use.

6. Combine all other ingredients in an attractive bowl and refrigerate at least one hour (best if kept overnight).

7. Serve bruschetta mixture with crisp bread slices on the side.

Nutritional information: 74.4 calories, <1 gram of protein, 10.1 grams of carbohydrates, 2.9 grams of fat, 0 milligrams of cholesterol, 299.3 milligrams of sodium, 1.7 grams of fiber, 17.1 milligrams of calcium, <1 milligram of iron

Allergen Notes and Additional Allergen Substitutions

- To make milk free, use dairy-free bread.
- To make egg free, use egg-free bread.
- To make soy free, use soy-free cooking spray.
- To make vegan, use vegan bread.

FODMAPs

- To make FODMAP friendly, toast the bread without garlic and onion powder, and substitute garlic-infused oil (page 31) for the fresh garlic and olive oil.

TIP: Try varying the base recipe with additional ingredients such as chopped roasted peppers and zucchini.

Cheese Puffs, Mini Knishes, and Pigs in a Blanket

My cocktail party favorites! The potato flatbread dough recipe (page 92) is used to make each of these terrific appetizers. I always have potato flatbread dough in the freezer so I can quickly defrost it and make these snacks any time.

Cheese Puffs SERVES 20

GF, SF*, NF*, PF, FF, SFF, V

½ batch of potato flatbread dough

4 ounces sharp cheddar cheese, cut into 20 pieces

1. Preheat oven to 350 degrees F.
2. Make 20 small balls of dough. Press a piece of cheese into each dough ball.
3. Bake on a baking sheet for 10 to 12 minutes, until golden.

Nutritional information: 64 calories, 2.9 grams of protein, 8 grams of carbohydrates, 2.6 grams of fat, 11.9 milligrams of cholesterol, 102 milligrams of sodium, <1 gram of fiber, 49.3 milligrams of calcium, <1 milligram of iron

Allergen Notes and Additional Allergen Substitutions

- To keep soy free, check the gluten-free all-purpose flour blend for soy and use butter and soy-free cooking spray or olive oil when making the dough.
- To keep nut free, check the gluten-free all-purpose flour blend for nuts when making the dough.
- To make milk free, use margarine when making the dough and use a dairy-free cheese.
- To make egg free, use a gluten-free, eggless egg substitute when making the dough.
- To make vegan, use margarine and a gluten-free, vegan egg substitute when making the dough and use a vegan, dairy-free cheese.

FODMAP Friendly

Mini Knishes SERVES 20

GF, MF*, SF*, NF*, PF, FF, SFF, V

½ batch of potato flatbread dough (page 92)

½ cup mashed potatoes

1. Preheat oven to 350 degrees F.

2. Make 20 small balls of dough. Fill each with about a teaspoon of mashed potatoes.

3. Bake on a baking sheet for 10 to 12 minutes, until golden.

Nutritional information: 46.9 calories, 1.8 grams of protein, 8.3 grams of carbohydrates, .9 grams of fat, 6 milligrams of cholesterol, 84 milligrams of sodium, <1 gram of fiber, 11 milligrams of calcium, <1 milligram of iron

Allergen Notes and Additional Allergen Substitutions

- To keep milk free, use margarine when making the dough.
- To keep soy free, check the gluten-free all-purpose flour blend for soy and use butter and soy-free cooking spray or olive oil when making the dough.
- To keep nut free, check the gluten-free all-purpose flour blend for nuts when making the dough.
- To make egg free, use a gluten-free, eggless egg substitute when making the dough.
- To make vegan, use margarine and a gluten-free, vegan egg substitute when making the dough.

FODMAP Friendly

Pigs in a Blanket   SERVES 20

GF, MF*, SF*, NF*, PF, FF, SFF

½ batch of potato flabread dough (page 92)

20 mini gluten-free hot dogs

1. Preheat oven to 350 degrees F.

2. Make twenty 1-inch dough balls (about ping pong ball size), push the mini hot dogs through the dough balls, and roll them to flatten and smooth out a little. Or pinch off a small piece of dough and roll in your hands to make a rope, wrap around each hot dog, and trim off any excess.

3. Bake on a baking sheet (seam side down if you wrapped them) for 10 to 12 minutes, until golden.

Nutritional information: 87 calories, 3.2 grams of protein, 8.3 grams of carbohydrates, 4.8 grams of fat, 13.5 milligrams of cholesterol, 190 milligrams of sodium, <1 gram of fiber, 10.9 milligrams of calcium, <1 milligram of iron

Allergen Notes and Additional Allergen Substitutions

- To keep milk free, use margarine when making the dough.
- To keep soy free, check the gluten-free all-purpose flour blend for soy and use butter and soy-free cooking spray or olive oil when making the dough. Check the mini hot dogs for soy.
- To keep nut free, check the gluten-free all-purpose flour blend for nuts when making the dough.
- To make egg free, use a gluten-free, eggless egg substitute when making the dough.

FODMAP Friendly

Crunchy Baked Chicken Tenders with Honey Mustard Dipping Sauce SERVES 6

GF, EF*, NF, PF, FF, SFF

Crushed waffles create an extraordinarily crispy crust with just a touch of sweetness.

For the chicken:

1 pound chicken tenders (cleaned of fat and veins, rinsed, and dried)

1 cup buttermilk (or 1 cup whole milk mixed with 1 tablespoon white vinegar)

1 teaspoon cayenne pepper

4 gluten-free frozen waffles, toasted

2 teaspoons dried Italian seasoning

½ teaspoon paprika

¼ teaspoon black pepper

Gluten-free cooking spray or 1 teaspoon olive oil

For the honey mustard dipping sauce:

2 tablespoons honey

2 tablespoons mustard

2 tablespoons olive oil

1. Preheat oven to 400 degrees F.

2. Mix chicken tenders, buttermilk, and cayenne pepper in a gallon-size sealable plastic bag. Place in the refrigerator for at least one hour.

3. Place waffles, Italian seasoning, paprika, and pepper in a food processor. Blend until coarsely crumbled. Spread on a baking sheet and bake at 350 degrees F for about 10 minutes to dry out. Place back in food processor and blend until finely crumbled.

4. Spread the crumbs out on a plate or a shallow dish. Place chicken in crumbs, a few pieces at time, and press crumbs onto chicken until both sides are well coated.

5. Spray a large baking sheet with cooking spray or grease with olive oil. Place chicken on baking sheet and bake for 10 minutes. Turn chicken over and bake for an additional 5 to 10 minutes, until cooked through.

6. *To make dipping sauce:* Blend all dipping sauce ingredients in a blender or food processor until smooth.

Nutritional information, chicken: 212 calories, 17.7 grams of protein, 16 grams of carbohydrates, 8.4 grams of fat, 56 milligrams of cholesterol, 252 milligrams of sodium, <1 gram of fiber, 26 milligrams of calcium, 1 milligram of iron

Nutritional information, honey mustard dipping sauce: 61 calories, <1 gram of protein, 5.7 grams of carbohydrates, 4.7 grams of fat, 0 milligrams of cholesterol, 115 milligrams of sodium, <1 gram of fiber, <1 milligram of calcium, <1 milligram of iron

Allergen Notes and Additional Allergen Substitutions

- To make soy free, use gluten-free, soy-free frozen waffles or substitute gluten-free, soy-free bread crumbs for the waffles and use olive oil or soy-free cooking spray.
- To make milk free, substitute rice, coconut, or almond milk mixed with 1 tablespoon white vinegar for the buttermilk.
- To keep egg free, check the waffles for egg.

FODMAPs

- To make FODMAP friendly, substitute gluten-free bread crumbs for the waffles and lactose-free, rice, or coconut milk mixed with 1 tablespoon white vinegar for the buttermilk. For the dipping sauce, substitute maple syrup for the honey.

TIPS: Freeze baked chicken tenders on a baking sheet, wrap individually in plastic wrap, and store in a freezer bag. To serve, bake on a baking sheet in a 350 degree F oven until hot and crispy. Serve with gluten-free barbeque sauce instead of honey mustard sauce.

Potato Pierogies SERVES 10

GF, NF, PF, FF, SFF, V

It took many tries to create the perfect pierogi dough, but it was worth the effort for these—soft and creamy on the inside, firm yet tender on the outside.

For the potato filling:

1½ pounds Yukon gold potatoes, peeled and diced

¼ cup low-fat sour cream

¼ cup milk

2 tablespoons chopped fresh chives

1½ teaspoons onion powder

¼ teaspoon mustard powder (optional)

For the dough:

2 eggs

¼ cup low-fat sour cream

¼ cup fat-free plain Greek yogurt

2 cups gluten-free all-purpose flour blend, plus extra for rolling out dough

½ teaspoon xanthan gum

2 teaspoons baking powder

½ teaspoon sea salt

Gluten-free cooking spray

2 tablespoons olive oil

¼ cup sliced green onions

1. *To make the filling:* Place potatoes in a large pot of water. Bring to a boil and cook for 15 to 20 minutes, or until potatoes are fork-tender. Drain and transfer to a large bowl.

2. To the bowl, add sour cream, milk, chives, and onion powder. Mash together using a potato masher or electric mixer until smooth and fluffy. Set aside.

3. *To make the dough*: Beat together eggs, sour cream, and yogurt in a large bowl until smooth.

4. Sift flour, xanthan gum, baking powder, and salt into the egg mixture. Stir until dough forms.

5. Knead dough on a lightly floured surface until smooth. Divide in half. Roll each half out to form a long rope and cut into 20 pieces. Roll each piece into a 2-inch circle about ⅛-inch thick.

6. Place ¾ of a tablespoon of the potato mixture onto each circle. Fold the dough over to form a semicircle. Seal edges with tines of a fork.

7. Bring a large pot of water to a boil. Boil the pierogies a few at time for three to four minutes (they are done when they float to the top). Drain.

8. Spray a large nonstick skillet with cooking spray. Add olive oil and heat over medium heat until oil shimmers. Place pierogies in skillet to brown, two to three minutes on each side. Drain on paper towels.

9. To serve, sprinkle with green onions and serve with additional sour cream, if desired.

Nutrition information: 232 calories, 5 grams of protein, 41.4 grams of carbohydrates, 6 grams of fat, 41 milligrams of cholesterol, 144 milligrams of sodium, 1.4 grams of fiber, 167 milligrams of calcium, 1.2 milligrams of iron

Allergen Notes and Additional Allergen Substitutions

- To make egg free, use a gluten-free, eggless egg substitute.
- To make soy free, use soy-free cooking spray.

TIP: Pierogies can be made ahead and frozen until ready to use. Freeze uncooked pierogies on a baking sheet and store in a freezer bag for up to six months.

 *Quick and easy*

Crispy Zucchini Sticks   SERVES 4

GF, SF*, NF*, PF, FF, SFF, V

Gluten-free cornflakes make a crispier coating than bread crumbs. I like to serve these with marinara sauce on the side (page 117).

Gluten-free cooking spray or 1 teaspoon olive oil

¼ cup tapioca flour

½ teaspoon sea salt

¼ teaspoon black pepper

1 egg

1 egg white

½ cup gluten-free cornflakes, finely ground

1 teaspoon onion powder

1 teaspoon garlic powder

2 tablespoons grated Parmesan cheese

1 tablespoon chopped fresh parsley

2 medium zucchini, unpeeled, cut into 3-inch sticks

1. Preheat oven to 425 degrees F. Spray baking sheet with cooking spray.

2. Mix tapioca flour, salt, and pepper in a sealable plastic bag.

3. Beat egg and egg white with fork in a shallow dish.

4. Mix cornflake crumbs, onion powder, garlic powder, Parmesan, and parsley in another shallow dish.

5. Place a few pieces of zucchini at a time in the bag with the flour. Shake to coat. Remove from flour and place in egg mixture before rolling in crumbs. Place on the prepared baking sheet. Repeat with remaining zucchini.

6. Bake in oven for 20 minutes, until browned and crispy.

Nutritional information: 78.9 calories, 3.9 grams of protein, 11 grams of carbohydrates, 2 grams of fat, 48.7 milligrams of cholesterol, 366.9 milligrams of sodium, <1 gram of fiber, 40.3 milligrams of calcium, <1 milligram of iron

Allergen Notes and Additional Allergen Substitutions

- To keep soy free, use olive oil or soy-free cooking spray and check the cornflakes for soy.
- To keep nut free, check the gluten-free cornflakes for nuts.
- To make milk free, omit the Parmesan cheese.
- To make egg free, substitute ⅓ cup gluten-free, eggless egg substitute for the egg and egg white.

FODMAPs

- To make FODMAP friendly, omit the garlic and onion powders and add 1 tablespoon of chopped green onions (green part only).

TIP: Reheat leftovers in a 400 degree F oven for 5 to 10 minutes. This will make them crispy again.

Cheesy Polenta Toasts with Roasted Mushrooms and Spinach SERVES 8

GF, EF, SF, NF, PF, FF, SFF, V

Polenta makes a perfect base for these veggies. Polenta is naturally gluten free, easy to make, inexpensive, and extremely versatile. Leave the polenta warm and creamy as an alternative to the toasts. Creamy polenta also can be served as a side dish with dinner or topped with poached eggs and served for breakfast, and it can be a great dessert when sprinkled with raw sugar and berries.

3 cups water

½ teaspoon sea salt

1 cup dry polenta

4 tablespoons olive oil, divided

2 tablespoons grated Parmesan cheese

1 (10-ounce) package baby portabello mushrooms, stems removed, cut in half

1 tablespoon balsamic vinegar

1 tablespoon minced garlic

¼ teaspoon sea salt

¼ teaspoon pepper

2 tablespoons chopped fresh parsley

¼ cup shredded Asiago cheese

1 (6-ounce) bag fresh baby spinach leaves

1 teaspoon garlic powder

1. *To prepare polenta*: Bring water and salt to boil in a medium saucepan. Gradually add polenta, stirring constantly with a whisk. Reduce heat to low and cook 15 to 20 minutes, stirring frequently, until polenta is thickened (it should come away from the sides of the pan and support a spoon).

2. Remove from heat. Stir in 1 tablespoon olive oil. Spoon polenta into a 9 x 9-inch square baking dish and chill for two hours, or until firm.

3. Invert polenta onto a cutting board. Cut into eight squares. Cut each square in half diagonally to form a triangle. Heat 1 tablespoon of the olive oil in a large

nonstick skillet. Add polenta to pan and cook five minutes on each side, until lightly browned. Sprinkle with Asiago cheese. Cover pan to let cheese melt.

4. *To prepare vegetables*: Preheat oven to 400 degrees F. Place mushrooms in a medium bowl and drizzle with 1 tablespoon olive oil, balsamic vinegar, garlic, salt, and pepper. Toss together and place on a baking sheet. Roast for 15 minutes, until mushrooms are tender. Set aside.

5. Heat 1 tablespoon olive oil in a large nonstick skillet. Add spinach and cook one to two minutes, until spinach is slightly wilted. Sprinkle with garlic powder. Remove from heat and set aside.

6. To serve, top polenta triangles with mushrooms and spinach.

Nutritional information: 180.8 calories, 5.1 grams of protein, 16.8 grams of carbohydrates, 10.2 grams of fat, 8.1 milligrams of cholesterol, 324.8 milligrams of sodium, 2 grams of fiber, 99.2 milligrams of calcium, <1 milligram of iron

Allergen Notes and Additional Allergen Substitutions

- To make milk free or vegan, use dairy-free or vegan cheeses.

FODMAPs

- To make FODMAP friendly, substitute eggplant for the mushrooms, omit the garlic and garlic powder, and use garlic-infused oil (page 31) in place of 2 tablespoons of the olive oil.

TIP: Use instant polenta to simplify this recipe and reduce preparation time.

Batter-Fried Onion Rings   SERVES 6

GF, SF, NF, PF, FF, SFF, V

These onion rings have a golden, crispy coating that you may have been missing in the gluten-free world. Dipping the onion rings in a rice flour mixture before coating with the batter gives them extra crunch.

1 large sweet onion, cut into ¼ inch slices

¾ cup white rice flour

½ cup tapioca flour

1 teaspoon gluten-free baking powder

½ teaspoon salt

1 teaspoon paprika

½ teaspoon xanthan gum

1 egg

1½ cups buttermilk (or 1½ cups whole milk mixed with 1½ tablespoons white vinegar)

½ cup water

¼ cup vegetable oil

½ teaspoon sea salt

1. Heat oil in a deep fryer to 365 degrees F or place 2 inches of vegetable oil in a deep pot and heat to 365 degrees F.

2. Separate the onion slices into ¼-inch-thick rings. In a large bowl, stir together the rice flour, tapioca flour, baking powder, salt, paprika, and xanthan gum.

3. Dip the onion rings into the flour mixture until they are coated. Set aside.

4. Whisk the egg, buttermilk, and water into the flour mixture. Dip the floured rings into the batter to coat then place on a wire rack until the batter stops dripping.

5. Deep fry the rings a few at a time for two to three minutes, or until golden brown. Drain on paper towels. Sprinkle with sea salt and serve immediately.

Nutritional information: 189 calories, 3.7 grams of protein, 20.5 grams of carbohydrates, 10.7 grams of fat, 65.8 milligrams of cholesterol, 291 milligrams of sodium, 1 gram of fiber, 118 milligrams of calcium, <1 milligram of iron.

Allergen Notes and Additional Allergen Substitutions

- To make milk free, substitute rice, coconut, or almond milk mixed with 1 tablespoon vinegar for the buttermilk and use ¼ cup of water.
- To make egg free, use a gluten-free, eggless egg substitute.
- To make vegan, substitute rice, coconut, or almond milk mixed with 1 tablespoon vinegar for the buttermilk, and use ¼ cup of water and a gluten-free, vegan egg substitute.

TIP: This recipe works well with zucchini sticks and squash blossoms.

Salads, Sides, and Soups

When I first went gluten free the only sides usually offered to me were salads, steamed vegetables, and baked potatoes. Boring. Over the years I have found ways to adapt all my favorite sides so I can enjoy a variety of exciting dishes—and now you can, too.

Pineapple Coleslaw

Beef and Spinach Salad with Caramelized Shallots

Mediterranean Salad

Rice Salad

Chopped Kale and Brussels Sprout Salad

White Bean Salad

Escarole and Beans

Rice-Stuffed Tomatoes

Creamed Spinach

Garlic Mashed Potatoes

Candied Carrots

Sautéed Garlic Green Beans

Elbow Pasta with Broccoli and Cannellini Beans

Baked Sweet Potato Fries

Sweet Potatoes with Chipotle-Honey Glaze

Creamy Seafood Bisque

French Onion Soup au Gratin

Hearty Tuscan Soup with Meatballs

Creamy Yellow Split Pea and Sweet Potato Soup

 *Quick and easy*

Pineapple Coleslaw   SERVES 8

GF, MF, NF, PF, FF, SFF, V

Pineapple adds a refreshing sweetness to this crunchy slaw, the perfect accompaniment to any BBQ meal.

6 cups shredded cabbage

1 cup shredded carrot

4 green onions, sliced

1 cup fresh pineapple, cut into small pieces

⅔ cup light mayonnaise

2 tablespoons apple cider vinegar

2½ tablespoons granulated sugar

½ teaspoon sea salt

¼ teaspoon black pepper

1. In a large bowl, combine cabbage, carrot, green onion, and pineapple.

2. In a small bowl, whisk together mayonnaise, vinegar, sugar, salt, and pepper.

3. Add dressing to cabbage. Toss to combine. Keep refrigerated until ready to serve.

Nutritional information: 93 calories, 1.1 grams of protein, 13.3 grams of carbohydrates, 4.5 grams of fat, 3.1 milligrams of cholesterol, 321.6 milligrams of sodium, 2.1 grams of fiber, 35.2 milligrams of calcium, <1 milligram of iron

Allergen Notes and Additional Allergen Substitutions

- To make egg free and vegan, use an egg-free mayonnaise.
- To make soy free, use a soy-free mayonnaise.

TIP: Save time by using a bagged coleslaw blend—found in the salad section of most supermarkets—and canned pineapple chunks, well drained.

 *Quick and easy*

Beef and Spinach Salad with Caramelized Shallots SERVES 4

GF, EF, SF, NF, PF, FF, SFF

This sizzling salad of sliced beef and shallots on a bed of spinach, drizzled with a tangy dressing, makes a light, protein-packed main dish.

For the dressing:

½ cup nonfat plain Greek yogurt

2 tablespoons olive oil

¼ teaspoon sea salt

¼ teaspoon black pepper

1 tablespoon horseradish

1 tablespoon gluten-free mustard

1 tablespoon chopped fresh chives

For the salad:

1 tablespoon olive oil

1 shallot, thinly sliced

1 large portobello mushroom, thinly sliced

1 (6-ounce) package fresh baby spinach

½ cup roasted red peppers, sliced

¾ pound flank steak, broiled to desired doneness and thinly sliced

1. *To make the dressing:* In a small bowl, combine yogurt, olive oil, salt, pepper, horseradish, mustard, and chives. Set aside.

2. *To make the salad:* Heat olive oil in a medium skillet over medium heat. Add shallot and cook until soft and browned, about five minutes. Remove from skillet.

3. In the same skillet, add mushroom and cook until softened. Remove from heat.

4. Divide spinach among four serving dishes. Top with shallots, mushrooms, red peppers, and steak. Serve with dressing.

Nutritional information: 363 calories, 28 grams of protein, 7 grams of calories carbohydrates, 24 grams of fat, 63 milligrams of cholesterol, 263 milligrams of sodium, 2.3 grams of fiber, 81 milligrams of calcium, 4.6 milligrams of iron

Allergen Notes and Additional Allergen Substitutions

- To make milk free, use a dairy-free yogurt.
- To make vegetarian, substitute canned, drained chickpeas for the steak.
- To make vegan, use a dairy-free yogurt and substitute canned, drained chickpeas for the steak.

FODMAPs

- To make FODMAP friendly, use lactose-free yogurt, substitute green onions (green part only) for the shallots, and omit the mushrooms.

TIP: Use a gluten-free, sliced, deli roast beef (such as Boar's Head) in place of flank steak to make this recipe even quicker and easier.

 *Quick and easy*

Mediterranean Salad   SERVES 4

GF, EF, SF*, NF, PF, FF, SFF

The Mediterranean diet is known for its heart-healthy benefits. This nutrient dense, satisfying salad is a complete meal by itself.

12 ounces grilled chicken cut into ½-inch slices

8 cups baby spinach

⅛ cup sliced black olives

¼ red onion, chopped

1 cup chickpeas, rinsed and drained

½ cup cherry tomatoes, either whole or cut in half

1 tablespoon olive oil

⅛ teaspoon sea salt

⅛ teaspoon black pepper

¼ teaspoon garlic powder

½ cup fat-free gluten-free Italian dressing

2 tablespoons Parmesan cheese

1. In a large bowl, combine spinach, olives, onions, chickpeas, and cherry tomatoes.

2. Drizzle salad with olive oil, sprinkle with salt, pepper, and garlic powder.

3. Toss salad with fat-free Italian dressing and layer chicken on the top.

4. Sprinkle with Parmesan cheese and serve.

Nutritional information: 286 calories, 34.6 grams of protein, 19.5 grams of carbohydrates, 7.8 grams of fat, 82.1 milligrams of cholesterol, 791.2 milligrams of sodium, 6.2 grams of fiber, 172.7 milligrams of calcium, 5 milligrams of iron

Allergen Notes and Additional Allergen Substitutions

- To keep soy free, check the Italian dressing for soy.
- To make milk free, omit the cheese.
- To make vegetarian, substitute grilled tofu for the chicken.
- To make vegan, omit the cheese and substitute grilled tofu for the chicken.

FODMAPs

- To make FODMAP friendly, substitute green onions (green part only) for the red onion and olive oil and vinegar for the Italian dressing.

TIP: Any kind of vegetable can be used in this salad. Try roasted red peppers, marinated green beans, cauliflower, broccoli, or asparagus.

 *Quick and easy*

Rice Salad SERVES 8

GF, MF, EF, SF, PF, FF, SFF, V, VG

Sesame oil adds a nutty taste to this refreshing, naturally gluten-free salad.

2½ cups water

1 cup uncooked brown rice

1 tablespoon sesame oil

⅓ cup dried cranberries

½ cup chopped red onions

2 stalks of celery, chopped

½ cup chopped walnuts

3 tablespoons chopped parsley

1 teaspoon sea salt

¼ teaspoon pepper

1. Boil the water with ½ teaspoon sea salt and sesame oil.
2. Add rice, lower flame, cover, and cook until all of the liquid is absorbed. If rice is undercooked add ½ cup additional water.
3. In a large bowl, combine cooked rice with all remaining ingredients.
4. Refrigerate until ready to serve.

Nutritional information: 169 calories, 2.9 grams of protein, 24 grams of carbohydrates, 6.8 grams of fat, 0 milligrams of cholesterol, 301 milligrams of sodium, <1 gram of fiber, 20 milligrams of calcium, 1.2 milligrams of iron

Allergen Notes and Additional Allergen Substitutions

- To make nut free, omit the walnuts.

FODMAPs

- To make FODMAP friendly, substitute ½ cup grapes, sliced in half, and 3 chopped green onions (green part only) for the cranberries and chopped onions.

TIPS: This salad can also be served immediately. Try using quinoa or millet instead of rice to add more vitamins, fiber, and protein.

 *Quick and easy*

Chopped Kale and Brussels Sprout Salad

SERVES 4

GF, MF, EF, SF, NF, PF, FF, SFF, V, VG

Kale and Brussels sprouts are superfoods loaded with nutrients and antioxidants. Toasted sunflower seeds, green apple, and celery add extra crunch to this satisfying salad. Everyone will be coming back for seconds.

2 tablespoons olive oil

12 ounces Brussels sprouts, cored and thinly sliced

4 cups chopped baby kale

1 medium green apple, chopped

1 celery stalk, chopped

¼ cup raw, shelled sunflower seeds, toasted

¼ cup olive oil

2 tablespoons balsamic vinegar

¼ teaspoon salt

¼ teaspoon pepper

1. Heat oil in a nonstick skillet over medium-high heat. Add Brussels sprouts to skillet and sauté for five to six minutes, until softened and lightly browned. Remove from heat.

2. Place kale, Brussels sprouts, apple, celery, and sunflower seeds in a large salad bowl. Toss to mix.

3. In a small bowl, whisk together oil, vinegar, salt, and pepper. Pour over salad and toss. Serve immediately.

Nutritional information: 300 calories, 7.5 grams of protein, 24 grams of carbohydrates, 21.8 grams of fat, 0 milligrams of cholesterol, 202 milligrams of sodium, 7.8 grams of fiber, 150.3 milligrams of calcium, 2.7 milligrams of iron

TIPS: Use a paring knife to core Brussels sprouts. Baby kale has small, tender leaves and a more delicate flavor than mature kale; it is a great addition to any salad because of its high nutrient value.

 *Quick and easy*

White Bean Salad SERVES 4

GF, EF, SF, NF, PF, FF, SFF, V

Beans are naturally gluten free and high in fiber and B vitamins, two nutrients that are often missing in a gluten-free diet.

¼ cup sun-dried tomatoes

1 (15-ounce) can small white beans, drained and rinsed

4 green onions, sliced

¼ cup chopped fresh basil

2 tablespoons sliced black olives

2 tablespoons reduced-fat feta cheese

¼ cup fresh lemon juice

1 teaspoon honey

½ teaspoon garlic powder

1 teaspoon dried thyme leaves

¼ teaspoon sea salt

¼ teaspoon black pepper

3 tablespoons olive oil

4 cups shredded romaine lettuce

1. Soak tomatoes in hot water until softened. Drain and chop.

2. Place tomatoes, beans, onions, basil, olives, and cheese in a medium bowl.

3. Whisk together lemon juice, honey, garlic powder, thyme, salt, pepper, and olive oil in small bowl. Pour over beans and stir gently to mix.

4. Place lettuce on a serving dish. Top with beans and serve.

Nutritional information: 249.4 calories, 9.4 grams of protein, 29 grams of carbohydrates, 11.9 grams of fat, 2.5 milligrams of cholesterol, 230 milligrams of sodium, 7 grams of fiber, 127.2 milligrams of calcium, 4.7 milligrams of iron

Allergen Notes and Additional Allergen Substitutions

- To make milk free, use a dairy-free cheese.
- To make vegan, use a vegan, dairy-free cheese and substitute agave or maple syrup for the honey.

TIP: This salad can be served warm. Heat the bean mixture and dressing on a stovetop or in a microwave until just warmed through, then serve over lettuce.

 *Quick and easy*

Escarole and Beans   SERVES 8

GF, MF, EF, SF, NF, PF, FF, SFF, V, VG

Via Italy, a classic favorite with a hearty flavor. Steaming the escarole before sautéing lowers the fat content of this recipe by using less oil. It tastes even better the second day, when the flavors have had more time to marry.

 2 heads escarole, washed and torn into pieces

 1½ tablespoons minced garlic

 3 tablespoons olive oil

 1 (10.5-ounce) can beans, such as kidney or cannellini, drained and rinsed

 1 teaspoon salt

 ½ teaspoon pepper

 Dash of dried red pepper

1. Steam the escarole until tender.

2. In a large skillet, sauté garlic in olive oil on medium-high heat until lightly golden.

3. Add the steamed escarole. Be careful: oil may splatter. Stir to combine with the garlic.

4. Add salt, pepper, and dried red pepper, adjusting to taste if needed. Add the beans, heat through, and serve.

Nutritional information: 88 calories, 2.7 grams of protein, 7.5 grams of carbohydrates, 5.3 grams of fat, 0 milligrams of cholesterol, 309.9 milligrams of sodium, 3.3 grams of fiber, 52.9 milligrams of calcium, <1 milligram of iron

TIP: Instead of escarole, try another leafy green vegetable such as kale.

 *Quick and easy*

Rice-Stuffed Tomatoes SERVES 6

GF, MF, EF, SF, NF, PF, FF, SFF, V, VG

Stuffed with seasoned rice instead of a buttery breaded filling, these tomatoes make an excellent light lunch. I like to make these in the summertime when tomatoes are at their peak of freshness and flavor.

1¼ cups water

½ cup uncooked white, jasmine, or brown rice

¼ cup olive or vegetable oil

1 tablespoon wine vinegar or lemon juice

1 teaspoon sea salt

¼ teaspoon pepper

1 tablespoon minced fresh parsley

2 tablespoons minced onion

6 medium tomatoes

1. Bring water to a boil. Add rice and a dash of salt. Cover and cook for 30 minutes, or until all of the water is absorbed. If too chewy, add a little more water and continue cooking until desired texture is achieved.

2. While rice is still hot, add oil to the pot and toss lightly. Add vinegar, salt, pepper, onion, and parsley. Toss lightly and let stand, covered, at room temperature for three hours.

3. At serving time, cut off top of each tomato, hollow out, discard the seeds, and mix the inside flesh of the tomato with the rice. Fill tomatoes with rice mixture and set on bed of lettuce. Serve at room temperature.

Nutritional information: 159.6 calories, 2.2 grams of protein, 17.4 grams of carbohydrates, 9.3 grams of fat, 1.3 milligrams of cholesterol, 374 milligrams of sodium, 1.7 grams of fiber, 18.8 milligrams of calcium, 1 milligram of iron

FODMAPs

- To make FODMAP friendly, substitute chopped green onion (green part only) for the chopped onion.

TIP: As an alternative to stuffing the tomatoes, seed and chop the fresh tomatoes and mix them with the rice.

 *Quick and easy*

Creamed Spinach   SERVES 4

GF, EF, NF, PF, FF, SFF, V

The perfect complement to any grilled chicken, steak, or seafood dish. Most creamed spinach is thickened with a flour roux. Instead, I use instant mashed potato flakes to thicken the sauce and add flavor.

16 ounces fresh baby spinach, stems removed

5 tablespoons light margarine

3 tablespoons finely chopped onion

1 garlic clove, crushed

1 cup fat-free half-and-half

2 tablespoons gluten-free instant mashed potato flakes

1½ teaspoons sugar

½ teaspoon salt

¼ teaspoon pepper

Dash of nutmeg

1. In a large skillet, heat butter over medium heat. Add onion and garlic and cook until golden.

2. Add the fat-free half-and-half and sugar. Stir until cream comes to slight boil. Whisk in the instant mashed potato flakes.

3. When sauce is smooth, add raw spinach. Stir and cook three minutes, until wilted down.

4. Season with salt, pepper, and nutmeg. If the sauce is too thin, add more potato flakes.

Nutritional information: 137 calories, 4.6 grams of protein, 13.2 grams of carbohydrates, 7.4 grams of fat, 60.3 milligrams of cholesterol, 604 milligrams of sodium, 2.9 grams of fiber, 172.5 milligrams of calcium, 3.6 milligrams of iron

Allergen Notes and Additional Allergen Substitutions

- To make milk free and vegan, substitute rice milk for the half-and-half and make sure the mashed potato flakes do not contain dairy (or use potato starch instead).

- To make soy free, substitute butter for the margarine and check the fat-free half-and-half and mashed potato flakes for soy.

FODMAPs

- To make FODMAP friendly, substitute chopped green onions (green part only) for the onions, 1 tablespoon of garlic-infused oil (page 31) for the garlic clove, rice milk for the fat-free half-and-half, and potato starch for the mashed potato flakes.

TIP: Potato starch can be used if mashed potato flakes are not available.

 *Quick and easy*

Garlic Mashed Potatoes   SERVES 10

GF, EF, NF, PF, FF, SFF, V

Boiling the garlic in the water with the potatoes softens the flavor.

3 quarts of water

1 teaspoon salt

8 medium russet potatoes, peeled and cubed

10 to 12 cloves garlic, peeled and smashed

1 teaspoon salt

¾ cup (12 tablespoons) light margarine, softened

¾ cup fat-free half-and-half

½ teaspoon fresh ground pepper

1. Bring water and salt to a boil. Add potatoes and garlic and cook for 15 minutes, or until potatoes are tender.

2. Drain the potatoes and garlic. Return the potatoes and garlic to the hot pot and mash with a potato masher. Add the margarine and blend into the potatoes. Stir in the fat-free half-and-half.

3. Season with salt and pepper. If potatoes are too thick or dry add more half-and-half.

Nutritional information: 252.5 calories, 2.9 grams of protein, 29.5 grams of carbohydrates, 14.1 grams of fat, <1 milligram of cholesterol, 467.7 milligrams of sodium, 2.7 grams of fiber, 35 milligrams of calcium, <1 milligram of iron

Allergen Notes and Additional Allergen Substitutions

- To make milk free, substitute rice milk for the half-and-half.
- To make soy free, substitute butter for the margarine.

FODMAPs

- To make FODMAP friendly, substitute half-and-half for the fat-free half-and-half and 2 tablespoons of garlic-infused oil (page 31) for the garlic cloves.

TIPS: If you like a more rustic mashed potato, use red potatoes and do not peel. Save the potato water and use it to thicken sauces, soups, stews, and gravies.

 *Quick and easy*

Candied Carrots   SERVES 4

GF, EF, SF, NF, PF, FF, SFF, V

Combining baby carrots with butter, honey, and brown sugar is the perfect way to get everyone to eat their vegetables and makes a great, naturally gluten-free side.

  1-pound bag baby carrots

  2 tablespoons butter

  3 tablespoons honey

  3 tablespoons brown sugar

  ¼ teaspoon sea salt

1. Steam carrots until tender. Transfer to a bowl and add the butter. Toss until butter is melted.

2. Add honey and toss. Add brown sugar and salt. Toss until carrots are well coated.

Nutritional information: 164.1 calories, <1 gram of protein, 28.9 grams of carbohydrates, 5.9 grams of fat, 15.2 milligrams of cholesterol, 274.1 milligrams of sodium, 3.3 grams of fiber, 44.8 milligrams of calcium, 1.1 milligrams of iron

Allergen Notes and Additional Allergen Substitutions

- To make milk free, use nondairy butter or olive oil.
- To make vegan, use nondairy butter or olive oil and substitute agave or maple syrup for the honey.

FODMAPs

- To make FODMAP friendly, substitute maple syrup for the honey and white granulated sugar for the brown sugar.

TIP: Add a teaspoon of orange zest or ginger for extra flavor.

 *Quick and easy*

Sautéed Garlic Green Beans   SERVES 4

GF, MF, EF, SF, NF, PF, FF, SFF, V, VG

Sautéing the green beans enhances their flavor.

   1 pound fresh crisp green beans, rinsed and ends trimmed

   3 tablespoons olive oil

   3 cloves garlic, sliced thin

   ½ teaspoon sea salt

   ¼ teaspoon fresh ground pepper

1. Lightly steam green beans until crisp-tender. Do not cook through.

2. Place green beans in an ice bath to stop the cooking process. Drain, then pat dry with a clean dish towel or paper towels.

3. Heat olive oil in a nonstick skillet over a medium heat. Add the garlic and sauté until just golden.

4. Add the green beans and toss with the garlic, salt, and pepper. Continue tossing until green beans are well coated and cooked through.

Nutritional information: 139.8 calories, 1.5 grams of protein, 7.5 grams of carbohydrates, 10.1 grams of fat, 0 milligrams of cholesterol, 275.7 milligrams of sodium, 2.7 grams of fiber, 58.7 milligrams of calcium, <1 milligram of iron

FODMAPs

- To make FODMAP friendly, omit the garlic and substitute 2 tablespoons of garlic-infused oil (page 31) for the olive oil.

TIP: This recipe also works well with asparagus, broccoli, spinach, and cauliflower.

 *Quick and easy*

Elbow Pasta with Broccoli and Cannellini Beans SERVES 8

GF, EF*, SF*, NF, PF, FF, SFF

There are so many excellent gluten-free pasta options available now. I find small shapes, like elbows, turn out best. Combining pasta with vegetables and beans ramps up the taste, texture, and nutritional value of the dish. This is a hearty side dish that can also serve as a complete meal.

½ pound gluten-free elbow pasta

1 head broccoli, cut into florets and steamed

½ cup gluten-free chicken broth

2 tablespoons olive oil

3 cloves garlic, sliced thin or chopped

1 (10.25-ounce) can of cannellini beans with liquid

Pasta water as needed

1 teaspoon kosher salt

⅓ teaspoon fresh ground pepper

¼ cup grated Romano or Parmesan cheese

1. Bring a large pot of salted water to a boil and cook pasta according to directions on package until al dente. Drain, reserving pasta water.

2. In a large skillet, sauté garlic in olive oil until brown. Add broccoli and cook for two to three minutes.

3. Add chicken broth and cannellini beans with liquid and bring to a simmer. If needed, add just enough pasta water to finish cooking the broccoli.

4. Add cooked pasta, salt, and pepper. Serve with grated cheese.

Nutritional information: 176 calories, 5.5 grams of protein, 28 grams of carbohydrates, 4.2 grams of fat, 2 milligrams of cholesterol, 406 milligrams of sodium, 4.2 grams of fiber, 62 milligrams of calcium, <1 milligram of iron

Allergen Notes and Additional Allergen Substitutions

- To keep egg free, check the pasta for eggs.
- To keep soy free, check the pasta and chicken broth for soy.
- To make milk free, use a dairy-free cheese.
- To make vegetarian, substitute vegetable broth for the chicken broth.
- To make vegan, substitute vegan vegetable broth for the chicken broth and use a vegan, dairy-free cheese.

FODMAPs

- To make FODMAP friendly, substitute spinach for the broccoli, 1 tablespoon of garlic-infused oil (page 31) for the garlic, and chickpeas for the cannellini beans. Use homemade chicken broth.

TIPS: If you like garlic, try doubling or tripling the amount in the recipe. Instead of broccoli, use asparagus, escarole, kale, broccolini, or a combination of these.

 *Quick and easy*

Baked Sweet Potato Fries   SERVES 4
GF, MF, EF, NF, PF, FF, SFF, V, VG

Sweet potatoes have more nutrients than white potatoes and work well as fries. This spice blend delivers a nice sweet and spicy kick.

- 2 medium sweet potatoes, rinsed and cut into thin wedges (remove peels if desired)
- ½ teaspoon onion powder
- ½ teaspoon garlic powder
- ½ teaspoon red pepper flakes
- 1 teaspoon sea salt
- 1 teaspoon sugar
- ¼ teaspoon ground cinnamon
- Gluten-free cooking spray

1. Preheat oven to 375 degrees F.
2. Mix all spices together in a large bowl.
3. Toss sweet potatoes in spices and coat well.
4. Cover a baking sheet with aluminum foil. Spray aluminum foil with cooking spray, and spread sweet potato mixture in one layer on cookie sheet.
5. Spray tops of sweet potato fries with cooking spray.
6. Bake in the oven until crisp, turning frequently and spraying when dry with cooking spray, about 30 minutes.

Nutritional information: 63 calories, 1.1 grams of protein, 14.8 grams of carbohydrates, <1 gram of fat, 0 milligrams of cholesterol, 586.4 milligrams of sodium, 2.1 grams of fiber, 23.8 milligrams of calcium, <1 milligram of iron

Allergen Notes and Additional Allergen Substitutions
- To make soy free, use soy-free cooking spray.

FODMAPs

- To make FODMAP friendly, substitute 1 tablespoon of garlic-infused oil (page 31) for the garlic and onion powders.

TIPS: Be careful not to overcook. If you like crispier fries bake them at 400 degrees F and toss more frequently. They should be done in about 20 minutes, depending on the size of your fries.

Sweet Potatoes with Chipotle-Honey Glaze

SERVES 4

GF, MF, EF, SF, NF, PF, FF, SFF, V

I can't get enough of these sweet potatoes! Developed by Chris Singlemann, the executive chef of Watermill Caterers, they are bursting with flavor. Make sure you use the chipotle powder to taste—it packs a real punch.

2 large sweet potatoes, peeled and rinsed

1 teaspoon salt

¼ teaspoon black pepper

Dash of chipotle powder to taste (very spicy)

2 tablespoons olive oil

1 teaspoon honey

1. Slice the sweet potatoes about ¼-inch thick, place in a pot of water and bring to a quick boil. Boil for one to two minutes, until slightly tender but still firm. Drain and season with salt, pepper, and chipotle powder.

2. Heat a skillet over high heat and add olive oil. When oil shimmers, add the seasoned sweet potato slices and allow them to sear. Once they start to caramelize, turn over, cook for another minute, then drizzle honey over top.

3. Continue to sauté as the honey glazes the potatoes. Serve immediately.

Nutritional information: 179.6 calories, 2.1 grams of protein, 28.2 grams of carbohydrates, 6.8 grams of fat, 0 milligrams of cholesterol, 654.7 milligrams of sodium, 4 grams of fiber, 41 milligrams of calcium, <1 milligram of iron

Allergen Notes and Additional Allergen Substitutions

- To make vegan, substitute agave or maple syrup for the honey.

FODMAPs

- To make FODMAP friendly, substitute maple syrup for the honey.

TIP: Try with maple syrup instead of honey.

Creamy Seafood Bisque   SERVES 8

GF, EF, SF*, NF, PF

Creamed soups are typically made with wheat flour, but I've found tapioca flour makes an excellent gluten-free alternative. Never use fake crabmeat as a substitute for real; it contains gluten.

3 tablespoons olive oil

½ cup chopped green onion

½ cup chopped celery

½ cup chopped carrots

3 tablespoons tapioca flour

4 cups gluten-free, unsalted seafood or chicken broth

3 medium white potatoes cut into ½-inch cubes

½ teaspoon salt

½ teaspoon pepper

1 cup half-and-half

6 ounces lump crab meat

10 ounces cooked small shrimp

½ cup roasted red peppers, chopped

2 tablespoons sherry

1 tablespoon chopped flat-leaf parsley

1. Heat olive oil in a large pot over medium heat. Add onion, celery, and carrots. Sauté for five minutes, until softened.

2. Whisk in tapioca flour until well combined. Whisk in broth.

3. Add potatoes. Reduce heat and simmer for 20 to 30 minutes until vegetables are tender.

4. Puree soup with an immersion blender. (If you use a regular blender, carefully puree a small amount at a time. Transfer back to pot.)

5. Slowly stir in half-and-half. Add crab, shrimp, red peppers, and sherry. Simmer until thickened. Sprinkle with parsley and serve hot.

Nutrition information: 198 calories, 15.3 grams of protein, 9.9 grams of carbohydrates, 10.3 grams of fat, 105 milligrams of cholesterol, 675 milligrams of sodium, 1.2 grams of fiber, 88 milligrams of calcium, <1 milligram of iron

Allergen Notes and Additional Allergen Substitutions
- To keep soy free, check the chicken or seafood broth for soy.
- To make milk free, substitute unsweetened coconut or rice milk for the half-and-half.

FODMAPs
- To make FODMAP friendly, omit the celery, use only the green part of the onion, and substitute unsweetened coconut or rice milk for the half-and-half.

TIP: Add any type of real seafood you like to this soup. Cod and lobster work very well.

French Onion Soup au Gratin   SERVES 4

GF, EF, NF, PF, FF, SFF

I love French onion soup and using gluten-free broth and bread make this a safe option. The classic recipe calls for Gruyère cheese, but I prefer to top this rich soup with a combination of Monterey Jack, mozzarella, and Parmesan. Be sure to caramelize the onions as it really sweetens and intensifies their flavor.

3 tablespoons olive oil

3 tablespoons unsalted butter

4 cups thinly sliced sweet onions (Vidalia onions are perfect)

1 (32-ounce) container gluten-free unsalted beef broth

1 teaspoon dried thyme leaves

1 bay leaf

½ teaspoon salt

¼ teaspoon pepper

1 tablespoon sherry

2 gluten-free ciabatta rolls, sliced in half

¼ cup Monterey Jack cheese, shredded

¼ cup mozzarella cheese, shredded

2 tablespoons shredded Parmesan cheese

1. Heat the oven broiler.

2. Melt butter with olive oil in a large stockpot over medium heat. Add onions and sauté until well browned, but not burned, about 20 minutes.

3. Add the broth, thyme, bay leaf, salt, and pepper. Simmer until the flavors are well blended, about 30 minutes. Stir in the sherry. Remove the bay leaf.

4. Place ciabatta slices on a baking sheet and toast under broiler until lightly browned.

5. Ladle the soup into individual ovenproof soup bowls. Top with one slice of the ciabatta and sprinkle with cheeses.

6. Place bowls on a baking sheet and broil until cheese is melted and bubbly. Serve immediately.

Nutrition information: 372 calories, 13.8 grams of protein, 23.6 grams of carbohydrates, 25 grams of fat, 43 milligrams of cholesterol, 714 milligrams of sodium, 3.6 grams of fiber, 290 milligrams of calcium, 1.3 milligrams of iron

Allergen Notes and Additional Allergen Substitutions

- To make milk free, substitute margarine for the butter and use dairy-free cheeses and rolls.
- To make soy free, use soy-free broth and rolls.
- To make vegetarian, substitute vegetable broth for the beef broth.
- To make vegan, substitute margarine for the butter and vegetable broth for the beef broth, use vegan, dairy-free cheese, and check the rolls for eggs and dairy.

TIP: Try different combinations of cheeses such as Swiss, provolone, and Parmesan.

Hearty Tuscan Soup with Meatballs   SERVES 8

GF, MF, SF*, NF, PF, FF, SFF

Small pasta shells and mini meatballs dot this rich vegetable soup.

For the soup:

> 1½ cups mixed green and yellow split peas, lentils, and white or brown rice
>
> 10 cups water or gluten-free vegetable or chicken broth
>
> 1½ teaspoons sea salt
>
> 2 carrots, diced
>
> 2 stalks celery, diced
>
> 2 cups shredded cabbage
>
> ¼ cup gluten-free tiny or small pasta, such as small shells (uncooked)

For the meatballs:

> 1 pound ground sirloin
>
> 1 egg
>
> ¼ cup uncooked Carolina white rice
>
> ½ teaspoon garlic salt
>
> ¼ teaspoon black pepper
>
> ½ teaspoon poultry seasoning

1. Combine first three soup ingredients in a slow cooker on high for two-and-a-half hours, until beans are soft.

2. While the beans cook, make the meatballs. Mix together all ingredients for meatballs and roll them into mini meatballs about the size of a ping pong ball.

3. Add the carrots, celery, cabbage, meatballs, and gluten-free pasta to the bean mixture.

4. Continue to cook for two hours on high heat. Add additional water or broth if too thick.

Nutritional information: 291 calories, 20.1 grams of protein, 37 grams of carbohydrates, 6.7 grams of fat, 60 milligrams of cholesterol, 550.3 milligrams of sodium, 7.7 grams of fiber, 48.9 milligrams of calcium, 3.5 milligrams of iron

Allergen Notes and Additional Allergen Substitutions

- To keep soy free, check the pasta for soy.
- To make egg free, use a gluten-free, eggless egg substitute and check the pasta for eggs.

TIP: This recipe also can be made in a covered pot on top of the stove. Just shorten the cooking time by about a half hour.

Creamy Yellow Split Pea and Sweet Potato Soup   SERVES 6

GF, MF, EF, SF, PF, FF, SFF, V, VG

This low-fat and flavorful soup will warm you from the inside and out. Store-bought or canned soups are generally high in sodium. Making your own is a healthier option.

1 teaspoon almond milk

¼ teaspoon ground cinnamon

Dash ground nutmeg

¼ cup raw shelled sunflower seeds

1 tablespoon olive oil

1 shallot, chopped

1 tablespoon grated fresh ginger

8 cups water

1 (16-ounce) package dried yellow split peas

3 small sweet potatoes, peeled and cut into ½-inch cubes

½ teaspoon salt

½ teaspoon black pepper

1. Preheat oven to 350 degrees F.

2. In a small sealable plastic bag, combine almond milk, cinnamon, and nutmeg. Add sunflower seeds and toss to coat seeds. Place on a baking sheet and bake for six to eight minutes, turning halfway. Remove from the oven and set aside.

3. Heat olive oil in a large pot over medium-high heat. Add shallots and cook, until lightly browned and soft, about five minutes. Stir in ginger and cook for one minute more.

4. Add the water, peas, sweet potatoes, salt, and pepper. Bring to a boil. Reduce heat, cover, and simmer for 60 to 90 minutes, until peas and sweet potatoes are tender.

5. Puree soup with an immersion blender, or puree in batches in a blender or food processor, until smooth and creamy. Garnish with sunflower seeds.

Nutritional information: 335 calories, 17.7 grams of protein, 54 grams of carbohydrates, 6 grams of fat, 0 milligrams of cholesterol, 210 milligrams of sodium, 19 grams of fiber, 53 milligrams of calcium, 3.5 milligrams of iron

Allergen Notes and Additional Allergen Substitutions

- To make nut free, substitute rice milk for the almond milk.

FODMAPs

- To make FODMAP friendly, omit the shallots, add 2 tablespoons of fresh chives after blending/pureeing the soup, and substitute rice milk for the almond milk.

TIP: Use butternut squash or pumpkin in place of the sweet potatoes.

Breads and Biscuits

I love warm, crusty breads spread with sweet creamy butter or dipped into a flavorful olive oil. And there is also nothing more pleasurable than the smell of freshly baked bread filling your home. Since baking gluten free is challenging, I modified and changed my recipes over and over until I came up with breads that are golden and crisp on the outside and light and flavorful on the inside. These gluten-free breads are just as delicious and memorable as gluten-containing versions. Try my golden French bread, naan bread, garlic knots, sweet Irish soda bread, and pizza crust to satisfy your wildest cravings.

Naan

Skillet Corn Cake

Irish Soda Bread

French Bread

Pull-Apart Rolls

Potato Flatbread

Garlic Knots

Pizza Dough

Naan SERVES 10

GF, SF*, NF*, PF, FF, SFF, V

Naan is an Indian flatbread that is well worth the extra effort to make. This recipe was created with Chris Singleman, executive chef of Watermill Caterers.

2½ cups all-purpose gluten-free flour (plus more for rolling)

1¼ teaspoons xanthan gum (do not use if flour blend already contains it)

½ teaspoon kosher or sea salt

¼ teaspoon cream of tartar

4½ teaspoons sugar

1 packet rapid yeast

⅓ cup plain gluten-free yogurt

3 tablespoons olive oil

1 egg plus 1 egg white

½ cup warm water

1. In the large bowl of a standing mixer with paddle attachment, add flour, xanthan gum, salt, cream of tartar, and sugar.

2. Mix on low speed to combine all ingredients. Add yeast and mix again.

3. Add the yogurt, olive oil, egg, and egg white. Mix on low speed until just combined. Slowly add the warm water in a steady stream. Once the water is fully incorporated, turn mixer to medium speed and mix for two to three minutes.

4. Slowly add additional flour until the dough thickens and pulls from side of bowl.

5. Remove from mixer and gently knead into a ball of dough, set aside in a bowl, lightly covered, to double in size, 35 to 40 minutes.

6. Divide dough into 10 equal pieces. Roll out each piece on a lightly floured board to an oval shape, about ⅜-inch thick.

7. Heat 1 tablespoon of olive oil in a skillet over medium heat. Place one rolled out piece of dough in a frying pan. Large blisters will form on bread. Continue cooking until golden brown, then flip to cook the second side until golden brown. Repeat process for other pieces of dough, adding additional olive oil as necessary to prevent the dough from burning.

Nutritional information: 231 calories, 3.7 grams of protein, 42.3 grams of carbohydrates, 4.6 grams of fat, 18.8 milligrams of cholesterol, 137.4 milligrams of sodium, 1.1 grams of fiber, 31.1 milligrams of calcium, <1 milligram of iron

Allergen Notes and Additional Allergen Substitutions

- To keep soy free and nut free, confirm gluten-free all-purpose flour blend is soy free and nut free.
- To make egg free, use a gluten-free, eggless egg substitute.
- To make milk free, use a dairy-free yogurt.
- To make vegan, use a dairy-free yogurt and a gluten-free, vegan egg substitute.

FODMAPs

- To make FODMAP friendly, use lactose-free yogurt.

TIP: This is the perfect bread to serve alongside dips, soups, and salads.

 *Quick and easy*

Skillet Corn Cake SERVES 9

GF, SF*, NF*, PF, FF, SFF, V

You won't miss the gluten in these moist corn cakes. Making them in the skillet gives them an extra crispy crust. It's like eating a large muffin top.

1 stick unsalted butter, softened

⅓ cup sugar

2 eggs

1 cup buttermilk (or 1 cup of whole milk mixed with 1 tablespoon white vinegar)

1 teaspoon vanilla extract

¾ cup gluten-free all-purpose flour blend

1 cup corn meal

1 teaspoon xanthan gum

1 teaspoon salt

1 teaspoon baking powder

Gluten-free cooking spray or 1 teaspoon olive oil

1. Preheat oven to 375 degrees F.

2. Cream together butter and sugar until fluffy. Add eggs, buttermilk, and vanilla extract and mix until well combined.

3. In a large bowl, combine other dry ingredients. Slowly beat into wet ingredients until uniform in texture.

4. Pour batter into four mini cast-iron skillet pans coated with cooking spray.

5. Bake until golden, about 20 minutes.

Nutritional information: 268 calories, 5.4 grams of protein, 34 grams of carbohydrates, 12.4 grams of fat, 70 milligrams of cholesterol, 328 milligrams of sodium, <1 gram of fiber, 44 milligrams of calcium, <1 milligram of iron

Allergen Notes and Additional Allergen Substitutions

- To keep soy free, check the gluten-free all-purpose flour blend for soy and use a soy-free cooking spray or olive oil to coat pans.

- To keep nut free, check the gluten-free all-purpose flour blend for nuts.

- To make milk free, substitute margarine for the butter and rice, coconut, or almond milk mixed with 1 tablespoon white vinegar for the buttermilk.

- To make egg free, use a gluten-free, eggless egg substitute.

- To make vegan, use a gluten-free, vegan egg substitute and rice, coconut, or almond milk mixed with 1 tablespoon white vinegar for the buttermilk.

FODMAPs

- To make FODMAP friendly, use lactose-free, rice, or coconut milk mixed with 1 table-spoon white vinegar for the buttermilk.

TIPS: Make corn muffins by pouring the batter into paper-lined muffin tins and baking for 20 minutes, until golden. You can also make a thinner corn cake by spreading batter in a 12 × 9 × 3-inch pan coated with cooking spray. Bake for 25 minutes, or until a toothpick comes out clean.

Irish Soda Bread SERVES 10

GF, SF, NF, PF, FF, SFF, V

What would Saint Paddy's day be without Irish soda bread? I've found bean flour provides the perfect texture and helps to hold the bread together nicely.

1 cup white rice flour

½ cup garbanzo bean flour

½ cup cornstarch

1 teaspoon xanthan gum

2 teaspoons baking soda

½ teaspoon cream of tartar

½ teaspoon salt

4 tablespoons unsalted cold butter

2 tablespoons granulated sugar

1 cup raisins

2 tablespoons caraway seeds

1 egg

½ cup buttermilk (or ½ cup of whole milk mixed with ½ tablespoon white vinegar)

1. Preheat oven to 375 degrees F. Line a baking sheet with parchment paper.

2. Sift all dry ingredients from white rice flour through salt into a large bowl.

3. Using a pastry blender, cut butter into flour mixture until mixture resembles coarse crumbs.

4. Stir in sugar, raisins, and caraway seeds.

5. In a separate bowl, whisk together egg and buttermilk. Stir into flour mixture and combine until a dough forms. Gather the dough with your hands, working it as little as possible. It will be crumbly. Place the round of dough on the prepared baking sheet. Cut an "X" into the top and place in preheated oven.

6. Bake the bread for 40 to 45 minutes, or until golden brown and firm. Remove from oven. Allow to cool before slicing.

Nutritional information: 218 calories, 4 grams of protein, 38 grams of carbohydrates, 6.2 grams of fat, 31.7 milligrams of cholesterol, 399 milligrams of sodium, 2.8 grams of fiber, 57.2 milligrams of calcium, 1 milligram of iron

Allergen Notes and Additional Allergen Substitutions

- To make milk free, substitute margarine for the butter and rice, coconut, or almond milk mixed with ½ tablespoon white vinegar for the buttermilk.
- To make egg free, use a gluten-free, eggless egg substitute.
- To make vegan, substitute margarine for the butter and rice, coconut, or almond milk mixed with ½ tablespoon white vinegar for the buttermilk, and use a gluten-free, vegan egg substitute.

FODMAPs

- To make FODMAP friendly, substitute ½ cup gluten-free flour blend for the garbanzo bean flour, substitute lactose-free, rice, or coconut milk mixed with ½ tablespoon white vinegar for the buttermilk, and omit the raisins.

TIP: Use frozen butter and grate into flour mixture. You can prepare the flour/butter crumb mixture and place in a sealable plastic bag in the freezer. Store for up to one month.

French Bread SERVES 20 (MAKES 2 LOAVES)

GF, SF*, NF*, PF, FF, SFF, V

Combining tapioca flour and potato starch makes a French bread so light that no one will ever think it is gluten free.

2 tablespoons sugar

2 packets rapid yeast

¼ cup warm water

1½ cups gluten-free all-purpose flour blend

1½ cups potato starch

½ cup tapioca flour

1 teaspoon xanthan gum

1½ teaspoons salt

2 eggs

2 tablespoons olive oil

2 teaspoons cider vinegar

¼ cup melted butter

1 cup sparkling water

1 tablespoon sesame seeds

Gluten-free cooking spray or 1 teaspoon olive oil

1. Preheat oven to 425 degrees F.

2. Dissolve yeast and half the sugar in ¼ cup warm water.

3. Line a two-loaf French bread pan with parchment paper and spray with cooking spray or drizzle with 1 teaspoon olive oil.

4. In a large bowl, mix together gluten-free flour blend, potato starch, tapioca flour, xanthan gum, and salt.

5. In a separate bowl, beat together eggs, remaining olive oil, cider vinegar, and melted butter. Add flour mixture, yeast mixture, and sparkling water. Beat until all ingredients are combined.

6. Scoop dough into three to four mounds on each side of the French bread pan. Flatten slightly with a wet spatula, spreading to connect the dough on each side of the pan into one long loaf.

7. Sprinkle dough with sesame seeds and slash several times with a knife across the top.

8. Bake for 30 to 35 minutes, until golden and loaves sound hollow when tapped. If bread is browning too much while cooking, cover with aluminum foil.

Nutritional information: 169 calories, 2 grams of protein, 28.3 grams of carbohydrates, 5.2 grams of fat, 27 milligrams of cholesterol, 223 milligrams of sodium, <1 gram of fiber, 4.7 milligrams of calcium, <1 milligram of iron

Allergen Notes and Additional Allergen Substitutions

- To keep soy free, check the gluten-free all-purpose flour blend for soy and use soy-free cooking spray or olive oil.
- To keep nut free, check the gluten-free all-purpose flour blend for nuts.
- To make milk free, substitute margarine for the butter.
- To make egg free, use a gluten-free, eggless egg substitute.
- To make vegan, substitute margarine for the butter and use a gluten-free, vegan egg substitute.

FODMAP Friendly

TIP: Try adding some flax, psyllium, or chia seeds for added flavor, nutrients, fiber, and variety. Add no more than ½ cup of any of these and reduce the gluten-free all-purpose flour blend by the same amount.

Pull-Apart Rolls SERVES 16

GF, SF*, PF, SFF, FF, V

Combining almond meal, potato starch, milk, and butter results in sweet, buttery rolls best right from the oven or lightly warmed.

1 cup warm milk

1 packet rapid yeast

¼ cup sugar

1 egg

2½ tablespoons salted butter, melted, divided

1 teaspoon cider vinegar

1 cup almond meal

1 cup potato starch

1 cup gluten-free all-purpose flour blend such as blend #2 (page xxiv)

1½ teaspoons xanthan gum

½ teaspoon sea salt

½ teaspoon poppy seeds

1. Preheat oven to 400 degrees F.

2. Mix together warm milk, yeast, and sugar. Let sit until foamy. Stir in egg, 1 tablespoon butter, and cider vinegar.

3. In a separate bowl, combine almond meal, potato starch, gluten-free flour blend, and xanthan gum.

4. Add dry ingredients to the yeast mixture and mix until well combined.

5. Coat a 9-inch round cake pan with ½ tablespoon butter.

6. Shape 16 dough rounds and place into the round cake pan, pushing together so they all fit. If they are too wet when shaping, mix in a little extra gluten-free flour blend.

7. Cover and let it rise in a warm place for one hour, or until doubled in size.

8. Brush the rest of the butter over rolls and sprinkle with sea salt and poppy seeds.

9. Bake 25 to 30 minutes, until golden.

Nutritional information: 148 calories, 4 grams of protein, 26 grams of carbohydrates, 3.7 grams of fat, 19 milligrams of cholesterol, 144 milligrams of sodium, 1.7 grams of fiber, 67 milligrams of calcium, <1 milligram of iron

Allergen Notes and Additional Allergen Substitutions

- To keep soy free, check the gluten-free all-purpose flour blend for soy.
- To make milk free, substitute rice milk for the milk and margarine for the butter.
- To make egg free, use a gluten-free, eggless egg substitute.
- To make nut free, substitute with additional gluten-free all-purpose flour blend for the almond meal.
- To make vegan, substitute margarine for the butter, substitute rice milk for the milk, and use a gluten-free, vegan egg substitute.

FODMAPs

- To make FODMAP friendly, use lactose-free milk.

TIP: Once baked, these rolls can be kept in the freezer for up to six months. Individually wrap in plastic wrap and store in a freezer bag. When ready to serve, defrost in the microwave for 10 to 15 seconds.

 *Quick and easy*

Potato Flatbread SERVES 10

GF, MF*, SF*, NF*, PF, FF, SFF, V

This combination of flours results in an easy to work with, soft, and flavorful dough. This bread can be used to make open-faced sandwiches or can be stuffed with fillings such as cheese or meat and then cooked. It's also great paired with your favorite dips and spreads.

1 large russet potato (about ¾ pound)

1 teaspoon sea salt

½ cup gluten-free all-purpose flour blend blend or brown rice flour, plus more for rolling

1 cup potato starch

2 teaspoons xanthan gum

½ teaspoon gluten-free baking powder

¼ stick (2 tablespoons) butter or margarine, melted

1 egg

2 teaspoons sugar

Gluten-free cooking spray or olive oil

1. Boil potato until just cooked; cool and peel. (If you prefer, you can cut up the potato and cook in the microwave in a small amount of water.) Place potato in food processor and process with salt until smooth.

2. In a bowl, combine gluten-free flour, potato starch, xanthan gum, and baking powder.

3. In another large bowl, combine butter with egg and sugar. Add potato mixture. Once well-combined, add gluten-free flour mixture. Add a little water if dough is too dry. Mix together until smooth.

4. Work dough into golf ball–size balls. If too sticky, add additional flour blend or potato starch. To loosen if too stiff, add a little of the water you used to boil or cook the potato.

5. On waxed paper that has been dusted with flour roll out each dough ball to make a ¼-inch-thick disk about 4 inches in diameter.

6. Spray a skillet with cooking spray or olive oil, then heat the pan over medium-high heat.

7. Cook each disk until brown and bubbling on each side. Serve warm.

Nutritional information: 161.4 calories, 1.9 grams of protein, 32 grams of carbohydrates, 2.9 grams of fat, 25 milligrams of cholesterol, 266 milligrams of sodium, 1.4 grams of fiber, 37 milligrams of calcium, <1 milligram of iron.

FODMAP Friendly

Allergen Notes and Additional Allergen Substitutions:

- To keep milk free, use margarine.
- To keep soy free, check the gluten-free all-purpose flour blend for soy and use butter and soy-free cooking spray or olive oil.
- To keep nut free, check the gluten-free all-purpose flour blend for nuts.
- To make egg free, use a gluten-free, eggless egg substitute.
- To make vegan, use margarine and a gluten-free, vegan egg substitute.

TIP: This dough holds up uncooked in the refrigerator for up to a week wrapped in plastic wrap.

Garlic Knots SERVES 20

GF, SF*, NF*, PF, FF, SFF, V

Crispy outside, chewy inside, these are delicious served with pasta or dipped into tomato sauce. Serve warm.

½ batch of potato flatbread dough (page 92)

1 tablespoon olive oil

1 tablespoon dried garlic

2 tablespoons Parmesan cheese

1. Preheat oven to 350 degrees F.

2. Roll dough into small balls. Then roll each ball into a long rope and shape into knots.

3. Bake for 10 to 12 minutes, until lightly browned. Remove from oven.

4. Heat oil in a frying pan over medium heat. Add garlic and baked knots and sauté until knots are well-coated with oil and garlic. Remove from heat and toss with Parmesan cheese.

Nutritional information: 161.4 calories, 1.9 grams of protein, 32 grams of carbohydrates, 2.9 grams of fat, 25 milligrams of cholesterol, 266 milligrams of sodium, 1.4 grams of fiber, 37 milligrams of calcium, <1 milligram of iron.

Allergen Notes and Additional Allergen Substitutions

- To keep soy free, check the gluten-free all-purpose flour blend for soy and use butter and olive oil when making the dough.

- To keep nut free, check the gluten-free all-purpose flour blend for nuts when making the dough.

- To make milk free, use margarine when making the dough and toss with a grated dairy-free cheese.

- To make egg free, use a gluten-free, eggless egg substitute when making the dough.

- To make vegan, use margarine and a gluten-free, vegan egg substitute when making the dough, and toss with a vegan, dairy-free grated cheese.

FODMAPs

- To make FODMAP friendly, use garlic-infused oil (page 31) instead of fresh garlic.

Pizza Dough   SERVES 8

GF, EF, SF*, NF*, PF, SFF, FF, V

No more soggy or heavy pizza dough! Allowing the crust extra time to rise gives you the perfect balance of crispiness and doughiness. Sunflower seeds give a nutty finish to this pie.

1 packet instant dry yeast

2½ teaspoons sugar

⅔ cup warm whole milk

⅓ cup plus 2 tablespoons corn meal, divided

⅓ cup tapioca flour or potato starch

½ cup gluten-free all-purpose flour blend

1 teaspoon baking powder

1 teaspoon xanthan gum

½ teaspoon sea salt

½ teaspoon onion powder

½ teaspoon Italian seasoning

2 teaspoons cider vinegar

3 tablespoons olive oil, divided

2 tablespoons rice flour for dusting

2 tablespoons toasted shelled sunflower seeds (optional)

1. Preheat oven to 425 degree F.

2. Mix together yeast, sugar, and warm milk. Set aside for 5 to 10 minutes, until bubbling.

3. In a large bowl, mix ⅓ cup corn meal, tapioca flour or potato starch, gluten-free flour blend, baking powder, xanthan gum, sea salt, onion powder, and Italian seasoning. Add yeast mixture, cider vinegar, and 1 tablespoon olive oil and work together into a dough ball. Let dough rest in the bowl, uncovered, for 10 to 15 minutes.

4. Dust work area with rice flour and roll dough into a 12-inch circle. If dough is too wet to roll, add extra rice flour.

5. Use remaining olive oil to coat a 12-inch pizza pan. Sprinkle with remaining cornmeal and sunflower seeds.

6. Shape dough onto pizza pan.

7. Let dough rest and rise for 30 minutes, uncovered.

8. Bake for 10 to 12 minutes.

9. Remove from oven and top pizza with desired toppings. Bake for an additional 15 to 20 minutes, or until set through and crust is golden.

10. If desired, brush crust edges with olive oil prior to serving.

Nutritional information: 196 calories, 4.5 grams of protein, 28.2 grams of carbohydrates, 7.5 grams of fat, 2.3 milligrams of cholesterol, 184 milligrams of sodium, 2.3 grams of fiber, 31.5 milligrams of calcium, <1 milligram of iron

Allergen Notes and Additional Allergen Substitutions

- To keep soy free and nut free, check the gluten-free all-purpose flour blend for soy and nuts.
- To make milk free and vegan, use a dairy-free milk.

FODMAPs

- To make FODMAP friendly, use lactose-free milk.

TIP: Crust can be premade, parbaked for 10 to 12 minutes, and refrigerated overnight until ready to top and finish baking, or it can be frozen, wrapped in plastic wrap and stored in a freezer bag, for up to six months. Uncooked dough can also be frozen when wrapped in plastic wrap and stored in a freezer bag.

Entrees

When it comes to developing gluten-free recipes, simple modifications can make the difference between a mediocre meal and one you can truly be proud of. Start by perfecting the obvious substitutions, such as gluten-free sauces and bread crumbs, and then experiment with creating flour blends and adjusting other ingredients. Since packaged gluten-free products can be higher in fat, I have modified these foolproof main dishes wherever possible to be lower in fat and sodium and higher in nutrients.

Sole Saint-Tropez

Tilapia with Salsa

Grilled Salmon with Balsamic Glaze

Orange Roughy Piccatta

Black Bean Burgers with Creamy Cilantro Pesto

Grilled Pork and Pineapple Kabobs

Garlic Chicken

Quinoa Pasta with Chicken Tenders

Chicken Cacciatore

Marinara Sauce

Linguini with Turkey Bolognese

Chicken Parmesan

Grilled Chicken with a Spicy Mustard Sauce

 *Quick and easy*

Sole Saint-Tropez   SERVES 4

GF, EF, NF, PF, SFF

This luscious cheese sauce has been modified to reduce the fat without sacrificing any of its richness.

1 pound filet of sole

3 tablespoons light margarine, divided

1 tablespoon grated carrot

½ teaspoon onion powder

½ teaspoon garlic powder

½ teaspoon salt

¼ teaspoon pepper

1½ tablespoons rice flour

½ cup fat-free half-and-half

¼ cup grated Gruyère cheese

¼ cup white wine

2 tablespoons chopped parsley

1. Preheat oven to 350 degrees F. Use 1 tablespoon margarine to grease a baking dish large enough to fit the fish.

2. Melt the remaining margarine in a large saucepan. Add the grated carrot and onion powder and cook gently until carrots begin to soften. Stir in garlic, salt, pepper, and rice flour until well combined.

3. Add fat-free half-and-half gradually to make a smooth sauce. Add the wine and heat until well combined.

4. Spread a little sauce in the bottom of the greased baking dish, arrange filets on top, and cover with the rest of the sauce. Sprinkle the top of the filets with grated Gruyère cheese.

5. Place fish in the oven. When the sauce begins to bubble (about five minutes), turn the oven temperature down to 300 degrees F and cook until the fish turns white. Baste if sauce does not cover fish.

6. Garnish with chopped parsley and serve.

Nutritional information: 228 calories, 25 grams of protein, 6.8 grams of carbohydrates, 9.4 grams of fat, 65 milligrams of cholesterol, 597 milligrams of sodium, <1 gram of fiber, 139.7 milligrams of calcium, <1 milligram of iron

Allergen Notes and Additional Allergen Substitutions

- To make soy free, substitute butter for the margarine and check the fat-free half-and-half for soy.

- To make milk free, substitute rice or coconut milk for the half-and-half and use a dairy-free cheese.

FODMAPs

- To make FODMAP friendly, substitute 3 tablespoons of garlic-infused oil (page 31) for the garlic powder, chopped green onions (green part only) or chives for the onion powder, heavy cream for the fat-free half-and-half, and grated Parmesan cheese for the Gruyère.

TIP: Try this recipe with chicken tenders or turkey cutlets and add an additional 5 to 10 minutes of cooking time.

Pumpkin Raisin Muffins with Pecan Streusel, page 14

Skillet Corn Cake, page 84

Beef and Spinach
Salad with
Caramelized
Shallots, page 50

Creamy Seafood Bisque, page 73

Carrot Cake with Creamy
Cream Cheese Frosting,
page 163

Cashew Butter Truffles,
page 145

Cinnamon Sugar Cookies,
page 155

Cranberry Almond Scones, page 19

Apple Crumb Pie, page 142

White Bean Salad, page 57

Naan, page 82

Homemade
Manicotti,
page 203

Rice-Stuffed Tomatoes,
page 60

Batter-Fried Onion Rings, page 45

Irish Soda Bread, page 86

Macaroni and
Cheese, page 186

Pizza Dough,
page 95

French Bread, page 88

Potato Pierogies, page 39

Pigs in a
Blanket,
page 36

Crispy Zucchini Sticks, page 41

Cheesy Polenta Toasts with Roasted Mushrooms and Spinach, page 43

Potato Flatbread, page 92

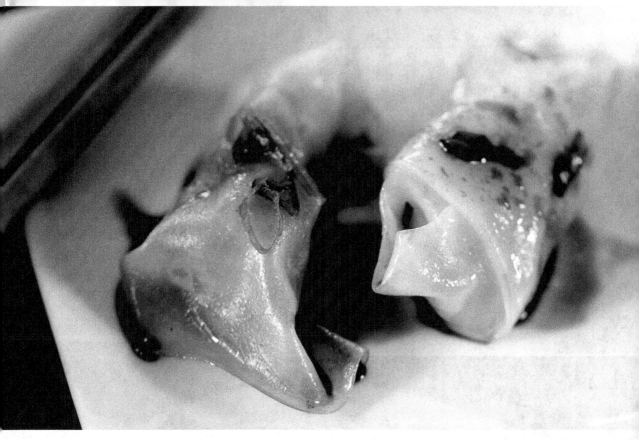

Pork Dumplings,
page 27

Pineapple Coleslaw, page 49

Oven-Baked "Fried Chicken," page 192

Pumpkin Tart with Bourbon Whipped Cream, page 152

Popcorn balls, page 144

Sausage and Cheese Biscuits, page 6

Stir-Fried Rice Noodles with Peanuts, page 176

Shepherd's Pie,
page 209

Peach Cobbler,
page 135

Tres Leches Flan
Cake, page 165

Homemade
Cheese Ravioli,
page 207

Cannoli Cones,
page 134

 *Quick and easy*

Tilapia with Salsa   SERVES 4

GF, MF, EF, SF, NF, PF, SFF

Tilapia is easy to prepare and has a very mild taste that works well with this bright, spicy salsa and many other recipes. It is also very low in fat.

>   1 pound tilapia
>
>   ½ teaspoon salt
>
>   ¼ teaspoon pepper

For the salsa:

>   2 cups chopped tomatoes, seeds removed, juices strained
>
>   1 celery stalk, chopped
>
>   ¾ cup chopped onions
>
>   1 green pepper, chopped
>
>   ⅓ cup finely chopped fresh cilantro
>
>   1 tablespoon chopped jalapeno peppers
>
>   2 tablespoons balsamic vinegar
>
>   1 teaspoon sugar
>
>   2 cloves garlic, chopped

1. Preheat oven to 350 degrees F.

2. Season tilapia with salt and pepper.

3. Mix together salsa ingredients.

4. Place tilapia in an oven-safe pan in a single layer. Top with salsa and place in the oven.

5. Cook for 10 to 15 minutes, or until tilapia is opaque all the way through.

Nutritional information: 155.6 calories, 24.2 grams of protein, 10.4 grams of carbohydrates, 2.1 grams of fat, 56.7 milligrams of cholesterol, 365.8 milligrams of sodium, 2.2 grams of fiber, 38.9 milligrams of calcium, 1.1 milligram of iron

TIP: Grouper, mahi-mahi, flounder, and catfish also work well in this recipe.

 *Quick and easy*

Grilled Salmon with Balsamic Glaze

SERVES 4

GF, MF, EF, SF, NF, PF, SFF

This sweet balsamic glaze pairs well with calcium- and omega-3 fatty acid–rich salmon; an especially good choice because many who have celiac disease have experienced poor calcium absorption. This dish can be an important addition to your diet.

1 pound salmon filet with skin

⅓ cup balsamic vinegar

⅓ cup white wine

1 tablespoon lemon juice

1 tablespoon dark brown sugar

¼ teaspoon sea salt

Dash of pepper

¼ cup chopped green onions

1. In a small saucepan, combine balsamic vinegar, white wine, lemon juice, and brown sugar. Boil, stirring continuously, until it reduces to less than half of the original volume, about 15 minutes.

2. Heat grill over medium heat. Sprinkle salmon with salt and pepper.

3. Grill salmon on both sides, finishing skin-side down on the grill. Cook until opaque in the center.

4. To serve, place salmon on a platter, drizzle with glaze, and sprinkle with chopped green onions.

Nutritional information: 180.9 calories, 25.8 grams of protein, 6.6 grams of carbohydrates, 5.1 grams of fat, 56.7 milligrams of cholesterol, 223.7 milligrams of sodium, <1 gram of fiber, 23.9 milligrams of calcium, <1 milligram of iron

FODMAPs

- To make FODMAP friendly, substitute granulated sugar or maple syrup for the brown sugar.

TIPS: Sear salmon in a skillet instead of a grill. To make your glaze thicker and the flavor more intense, cook it down a little longer.

 *Quick and easy*

Orange Roughy Piccata SERVES 4

GF, EF, NF, PF, SFF

Orange roughy is an excellent fish to sauté because it is firm enough to make a nice crust but stays juicy in the center. After trying many different gluten-free flours, I have found that rice flour works best for coating fish and poultry.

1 pound orange roughy

¼ cup rice flour

Gluten-free cooking spray

2 teaspoons butter

¼ cup white wine

¼ cup water

2 tablespoons capers

¼ cup lemon juice

Lemon wedges and parsley (optional)

1. Dredge orange roughy in rice flour.
2. Spray cooking spray in a sauté pan and heat pan over medium heat.
3. Place fish in sauté pan, rough side down. Brown fish slowly on both sides, remove from pan, and set aside.
4. To pan, add butter, wine, water, and capers and heat until mixture simmers.
5. Return fish to pan and cook until fish is opaque throughout. Add lemon juice and serve. Garnish with lemon and parsley sprigs.

Nutritional information: 155.7 calories, 19.3 grams of protein, 9.5 grams of carbohydrates, 2.9 grams of fat, 73.1 milligrams of cholesterol, 216.8 milligrams of sodium, <1 gram of fiber, 15.7 milligrams of calcium, 1.3 milligrams of iron

Allergen Notes and Additional Allergen Substitutions

- To make milk free, substitute margarine for the butter.
- To make soy free, use soy-free cooking spray.

FODMAPs Friendly

TIP: Cod and mahi-mahi also work well in this recipe.

Black Bean Burgers with Creamy Cilantro Pesto   SERVES 4

GF, SF*, NF, PF, FF, SFF, V

A hearty burger with bold flavors! There aren't many premade, gluten-free veggie burgers available, so this is a handy meat-free recipe to have on hand. Beans are loaded with water-soluble fiber that may help to lower your cholesterol.

For the burgers:

1 (16-ounce) can black beans, drained and rinsed

½ red bell pepper

½ onion

1 clove garlic, peeled and crushed

2 tablespoons green chilies

¼ cup fresh cilantro leaves

2 egg whites

1 teaspoon chili powder

1 teaspoon cumin

⅔ cup gluten-free bread crumbs

1 avocado, sliced

Lime wedges

Gluten-free cooking spray or 1 teaspoon olive oil

For the pesto:

2 cups fresh cilantro leaves

⅓ cup unsalted pumpkin seeds

1 clove garlic

2 tablespoons fresh lime juice

½ teaspoon salt

2 tablespoons olive oil

2 tablespoons water

¼ cup nonfat plain Greek yogurt

1. *To make the burgers:* In a medium bowl, mash black beans with a potato masher or fork until thick and pasty.

2. In a food processor, finely chop red pepper, onion, garlic, green chilies, and cilantro. Stir into mashed beans.

3. Mix in egg, chili powder, and cumin. Add gluten-free bread crumbs and mix until mixture is sticky, but not too wet, and holds together. Form into four patties. Place on a baking sheet lined with parchment paper and refrigerate for one hour.

4. Heat a grill pan over medium heat. Spray with cooking spray and grill patties for 8 to 10 minutes on each side.

5. *To make pesto:* Combine cilantro, seeds, garlic, lime juice, and salt in a food processor and pulse until coarsely chopped. With food processor running, slowly pour oil through feed tube, stopping halfway to stir. Add yogurt and blend until well mixed.

6. To assemble, top burgers with sliced avocado and creamy cilantro pesto. Serve with lime wedges.

Nutritional information, burgers: 362.8 calories, 14.9 grams of protein, 37.3 grams of carbohydrates, 18.3 grams of fat, <1 milligram of cholesterol, 584 milligrams of sodium, 7.6 grams of fiber, 8.4 milligrams of calcium, 3.2 milligrams of iron

Nutritional information, pesto: 136 calories, 5.1 grams of protein, 2.9 grams of carbohydrates, 12.4 grams of fat, <1 milligram of cholesterol, 300 milligrams of sodium, <1 gram of fiber, 2.9 milligrams of calcium, 1.2 milligrams of iron

Allergen Notes and Additional Allergen Substitutions

- To keep soy free, check the gluten-free bread crumbs for soy and use olive oil or soy-free cooking spray.
- To make milk free, check the gluten-free bread crumbs for milk and use a dairy-free plain yogurt in the pesto recipe.

- To make egg free, check the gluten-free bread crumbs for egg and substitute a gluten-free, eggless egg substitute for the egg whites.

- To make vegan, substitute a gluten-free, vegan egg substitute for the egg whites, check the gluten-free bread crumbs for milk and eggs, and use a dairy-free plain yogurt in the pesto recipe.

TIPS: Burgers can be baked in the oven at 375 degrees F for about 10 minutes on each side. This pesto adds a punch of flavor to chicken, fish, or beef.

Grilled Pork and Pineapple Kabobs   SERVES 4

GF, MF, EF, NF, PF, FF, SFF

No need to scour labels any longer. Here is a gluten-free teriyaki sauce that is sure to please.

1 pound of pork loin

½ cup fresh pineapple chunks, about 2 inches each

1 teaspoon garlic powder

½ teaspoon onion powder

For the teriyaki sauce:

2 tablespoons gluten-free soy sauce

1 tablespoon sugar

2 teaspoons cider vinegar

1 tablespoon garlic-infused oil (page 31)

1 teaspoon sesame oil

Dash of pepper

4 long metal skewers

1. Cut pork into 2-inch pieces and thread on metal skewers, alternating with chunks of pineapple. Sprinkle kabobs with garlic and onion powder. Arrange in a dish.

2. *To make the teriyaki sauce:* Combine all ingredients until sugar dissolves.

3. Cover kebabs with teriyaki sauce. Refrigerate for a half hour.

4. Grill over medium-high heat for five minutes, or until pork is cooked through and white in the center.

Nutritional information: 233.5 calories, 23.5 grams of protein, 7.2 grams of carbohydrates, 11.5 grams of fat, 73.7 milligrams of cholesterol, 452 milligrams of sodium, <1 gram of fiber, 22.2 milligrams of calcium, <1 milligram of iron

FODMAPs

- To make FODMAP friendly, substitute 1 tablespoon of garlic-infused oil (page 31) for the garlic powder and omit the onion powder. Add two chopped green onions (green part only) to the teriyaki sauce.

TIP: This recipe also works well with shrimp, tuna, and chicken.

Garlic Chicken   SERVES 8

GF, EF, SF*, NF, PF, FF, SFF

This is my favorite roast chicken recipe, marrying garlic, rosemary, and thyme.

1 whole (4-pound) chicken, cut into 8 serving pieces, skin removed

1 teaspoon sea salt

½ teaspoon freshly ground pepper

2 tablespoons olive oil

15 to 20 cloves garlic, peeled

1 tablespoon minced fresh rosemary

1 tablespoon minced fresh thyme

Zest of 2 lemons

¼ cup white wine

¾ cup gluten-free chicken broth

2 tablespoons unsalted butter at room temperature

1. Preheat oven to 400 degrees F.

2. Season chicken with salt and pepper.

3. Warm olive oil in a large Dutch oven (or large pot with lid) over medium-high heat. Brown chicken, in batches, for two to three minutes per side. Transfer the chicken to a plate.

4. Add garlic to the Dutch oven and cook, stirring, for one minute.

5. Remove the Dutch oven from the heat and add chicken, rosemary, thyme, and zest. Stir to combine. Cover the Dutch oven and roast for 20 minutes, basting the chicken occasionally with accumulated juices.

6. Uncover chicken and continue roasting until the chicken is cooked, about 30 minutes. Transfer chicken to a platter, leaving garlic in the Dutch oven. Cover the chicken loosely with foil.

7. In the Dutch oven, over medium heat, mash the garlic, add the wine, and cook for three minutes. Add the broth and cook, stirring occasionally, until slightly thickened, about five minutes. Whisk in the butter a little at a time. Season with salt and pepper.

8. Transfer sauce to a sauceboat and serve alongside chicken.

Nutritional information: 269.9 calories, 22 grams of protein, 2.3 grams of carbohydrates, 18.5 grams of fat, 92 milligrams of cholesterol, 453 milligrams of sodium, <1 gram of fiber, 24 milligrams of calcium, 1 milligram of iron

Allergen Notes and Additional Allergen Substitutions

- To keep soy free, check the broth for soy.
- To make milk free, substitute margarine for the butter.

TIP: Other herbs that can be used in place of the rosemary or thyme in this recipe include basil, oregano, cumin, or turmeric.

Quinoa Pasta with Chicken Tenders   SERVES 6

GF, EF*, NF*, PF, FF, SFF

Quinoa pasta, high in protein and fiber, is an excellent gluten-free pasta option. And who doesn't love juicy chicken tenders?

½ pound cooked quinoa pasta, drained

12 ounces chicken tenders, cleaned of fat and veins, rinsed, and dried

⅓ cup gluten-free all-purpose flour blend

1 tablespoon olive oil

2 tablespoons light margarine, divided

1½ cups mushroom, cut into quarters

4 cloves garlic, sliced

5 ounces fresh spinach

½ teaspoon salt

¼ teaspoon pepper

14 ounces plum tomatoes (not in sauce), chopped

1 cup gluten-free chicken broth

4 fresh basil leaves

¼ cup grated Romano cheese

1. Dredge chicken tenders in gluten-free flour blend. In a frying pan, heat olive oil over medium heat and lightly brown chicken on both sides (do not completely cook). Remove to a platter.

2. Add 1 tablespoon margarine to pan, add mushrooms and sauté over medium-high heat. Add sliced garlic and continue to sauté until the garlic starts to brown lightly.

3. Add the spinach, salt, and pepper and sauté. Add tomatoes and partially cooked chicken and toss to combine. Add broth, remaining margarine, and basil.

4. Serve over quinoa pasta sprinkled with Romano cheese.

Nutritional information: 325 calories, 19.7 grams of protein, 44 grams of carbohydrates, 7.5 grams of fat, 49 milligrams of cholesterol, 309 milligrams of sodium, 4.1 grams of fiber, 78 milligrams of calcium, 1.5 milligrams of iron

Allergen Notes and Additional Allergen Substitutions

- To keep egg free, check the pasta for eggs.
- To keep nut free, check the gluten-free all-purpose flour and pasta for nuts.
- To make milk free, use dairy-free cheese and check the pasta and gluten-free all-purpose flour blend for milk.
- To make soy free, substitute butter for the margarine and check the broth, gluten-free all-purpose flour blend, and pasta for soy.
- To make vegetarian, omit the chicken, use vegetable broth, and double up on vegetables.
- To make vegan, omit the chicken, use vegetable broth, double up on vegetables, and use a vegan, dairy-free cheese.

TIP: If the sauce is too dry, use some reserved pasta water to extend it.

Chicken Cacciatore   SERVES 6

GF, MF, EF, NF, PF, FF, SFF

This rustic Italian favorite of chicken and vegetables braised in tomato sauce is the perfect one-pot meal and is easy to make ahead.

2 tablespoons vegetable oil

3 pounds whole chicken, cut up

¼ teaspoon sea salt

¼ teaspoon black pepper

1 onion, thinly sliced

1 green bell pepper, thinly sliced

1 red bell pepper, thinly sliced

2 cloves garlic, minced

½ cup dry white wine or gluten-free chicken broth

1 (14-ounce) can diced tomatoes

1 (8-ounce) can tomato sauce

1 teaspoon dried oregano

¼ cup chopped fresh parsley

1. Preheat oven to 375 degrees F.

2. Heat oil in a large nonstick skillet over medium-high heat. Sprinkle chicken with salt and pepper. Place in skillet and brown well on both sides, about four minutes per side. Place chicken in a 9 × 13-inch casserole dish.

3. Add onions, peppers, and garlic to skillet and sauté for two to three minutes. Add wine or broth and cook for two minutes. Add diced tomatoes, tomato sauce, and oregano. Stir together and pour over chicken.

4. Cover with foil and bake for 45 minutes. Remove foil and bake an additional 15 minutes, or until chicken is cooked through and starting to fall apart.

5. Sprinkle with parsley and serve.

Nutritional Information: 232.4 calories, 26.8 grams of protein, 12.9 grams of carbohydrates, 8.4 grams of fat, 79.3 milligrams of cholesterol, 461.6 milligrams of sodium, 2.9 grams of fiber, 53.3 milligrams of calcium, 2.2 milligrams of iron

Allergen Notes and Additional Allergen Substitutions

- To make soy free, use soy-free vegetable oil and check the broth for soy.

FODMAPs

- To make FODMAP friendly, substitute two red peppers for the green pepper, 1 tablespoon of garlic-infused oil (page 31) for the garlic, and three green onions (green part only) for the onion.

TIP: This can be made in a slow cooker. Combine all ingredients and cook for eight hours on low.

Marinara Sauce   SERVES 6

GF, EF, SF, NF, PF, FF, SFF, V

Homemade marinara sauce is easy to prepare, uses basic pantry ingredients, and tastes so much better than store-bought versions. It is an easy topping for pasta, base for pizza, or dipping sauce for zucchini sticks (page 41). The possibilities are endless—and it freezes beautifully.

2 tablespoons olive oil

2 tablespoons minced garlic

1 medium onion, finely chopped

1 (28-ounce) can crushed tomatoes, such as San Marzano

3 teaspoons sugar

2 tablespoons chopped fresh oregano

½ teaspoon sea salt

¼ teaspoon pepper

3 tablespoons Parmesan cheese

1. Heat the oil in a large pot over medium heat. Add the garlic and sauté for two minutes.

2. Add onion and sauté until onion is translucent.

3. Add tomatoes, sugar, and oregano. Simmer over a low heat for 30 to 40 minutes, or until sauce reaches desired thickness.

4. Season with salt and pepper. Stir in Parmesan cheese.

Nutritional information: 129.3 calories, 3.4 grams of protein, 14.1 grams of carbohydrates, 5.7 grams of fat, 2.2 milligrams of cholesterol, 539.9 milligrams of sodium, 2.6 grams of fiber, 39.6 milligrams of calcium, 1.2 milligrams of iron

Allergen Notes and Additional Allergen Substitutions

- To make milk free and vegan, omit the Parmesan.

FODMAPs

- To make FODMAP friendly, substitute 2 tablespoons of garlic-infused oil (page 31) for the garlic and three chopped green onions (green part only) for the onion.

TIPS: Try adding fresh chopped thyme, parsley, and basil to taste for additional layers of flavor. Or, in step 4, add some potato vodka and heavy cream to taste to create a vodka sauce, or olives, capers, and red pepper flakes to create a puttanesca sauce.

Linguini with Turkey Bolognese SERVES 8

GF, EF*, SF*, NF, PF, FF, SFF

My healthier version of a traditional Bolognese. Browned turkey adds rich flavor to a basic marinara sauce (page 117), without the extra saturated fat of beef. This thick and hearty sauce also pairs well with cheese ravioli (page 207). I think rice pasta works best in this recipe since it's lighter than the corn or quinoa pasta, but be careful not to overcook.

Marinara sauce (page 117)

2 tablespoons olive oil

1 tablespoon minced garlic

1 medium onion, chopped

1 (6-ounce) can tomato paste

¾ pound (12 ounces) ground breast of turkey

1 teaspoon dried oregano or 2 tablespoons minced fresh oregano

1 bay leaf

¼ cup red wine

8 cups cooked gluten-free linguini

4 tablespoons Parmesan cheese

1. In a large pot, heat olive oil over low heat and sauté garlic for two to three minutes. Add onion and cook for about five minutes, until onion has just started to soften.

2. Add tomato paste and sauté for 8 to10 minutes. If pan is too dry and ingredients are burning, add a little water.

3. Add turkey, oregano, and bay leaf and cook until turkey is just cooked and white throughout.

4. To this mixture, add wine and marinara sauce, cover, and simmer for 30 to 40 minutes, until sauce reaches desired thickness. If too thick, add a little water to thin. Remove bay leaf.

5. Serve over linguini sprinkled with Parmesan cheese.

Nutritional information: 395.7 calories, 18.8 grams of protein, 58.1 grams of carbohydrates, 8.9 grams of fat, 24.4 milligrams of cholesterol, 642.4 milligrams of sodium, 5.3 grams of fiber, 75 milligrams of calcium, 3.1 milligrams of iron

Allergen Notes and Additional Allergen Substitutions

- To keep egg free, check the pasta for eggs.
- To keep soy free, check the pasta for soy.
- To make milk free, use a dairy-free cheese.

TIP: Add low-fat sausage pieces to bump up the flavor and texture.

Chicken Parmesan SERVES 4

GF, NF, PF, FF, SFF

Gluten free and lower in fat than traditional preparations, this recipe is very versatile. Try it with turkey or pork loin cutlets, flounder or tilapia filets, or butterflied shrimp.

1 pound chicken tenders, cleaned of fat and veins, rinsed and dried

¼ cup egg whites

⅔ cup gluten-free bread crumbs

½ teaspoon dried oregano or basil or gluten-free Italian seasoning blend

1 teaspoon garlic powder

½ teaspoon onion powder

Gluten-free cooking spray

1 cup marinara sauce (page 117)

2 tablespoons Parmesan cheese

½ cup shredded fat-free mozzarella cheese

1. Preheat oven to broil. Cover a baking sheet with aluminum foil and spray it with cooking spray.

2. Place one layer of chicken between two sheets of plastic wrap and pound until about ¼-inch thick.

3. Mix together bread crumbs, oregano, garlic, and onion powder.

4. Dip chicken into egg whites and then dredge through bread crumb mixture, coating both sides.

5. Place breaded chicken in a single layer on the baking sheet. Spray the top of the chicken with cooking spray.

6. Place the chicken in the oven, with the rack set in the middle, and broil chicken on high until browned on one side. Turn and brown the other side. Remove chicken from oven and set aside.

7. Turn oven temperature down to 400 degrees F.

8. Spread a ¼ cup marinara sauce in a casserole dish and top with chicken cutlets. Pour remaining tomato sauce over chicken and sprinkle with Parmesan and mozzarella cheese. Bake for 10 to 15 minutes, until sauce is hot and cheese is melted.

Nutritional information: 284.6 calories, 33.8 grams of protein, 18.9 grams of carbohydrates, 7.8 grams of fat, 87.5 milligrams of calcium, 673.1 milligrams of sodium, 4 grams of fiber, 195.5 milligrams of calcium, 2.2 milligrams of iron

Allergen Notes and Additional Allergen Substitutions

- To make milk free, check the bread crumbs for milk and use dairy-free cheeses.
- To make egg free, use a gluten-free, eggless egg substitute.
- To make soy free, check the bread crumbs for soy and use soy-free cooking spray.

FODMAPs

- To make FODMAP friendly, substitute 1 tablespoon of garlic-infused oil (page 31) for the garlic and onion powders and follow the FODMAP substitutions for the marinara sauce.

TIP: Baked chicken cutlets can be wrapped in plastic and frozen for up to six months.

Grilled Chicken with Spicy Mustard Sauce   SERVES 4

GF, NF, PF, FF, SFF

Try this for your next barbeque! Chicken cutlets are low in fat and gluten-free hamburger rolls are widely available, so dig in.

1 pound skinless, boneless chicken cutlets cut into 4 equal cutlets

1 tablespoon olive oil

1 tablespoon minced garlic

½ teaspoon onion powder

¼ teaspoon pepper

¼ teaspoon salt

4 gluten-free hamburger rolls

1 sliced tomato

4 thin slices red onion

For the spicy mustard sauce:

2 tablespoons brown mustard

2 teaspoons honey

1 teaspoon granulated sugar

1 tablespoon apple juice

2 teaspoons red pepper flakes (or to taste)

1. *To make spicy mustard sauce:* Combine mustard, honey, granulated sugar, apple juice, and red pepper flakes and refrigerate until ready to serve.

2. Place chicken, olive oil, minced garlic, onion powder, pepper, and salt in a sealable plastic bag and allow to marinate in the refrigerator for at least one hour.

3. Grill chicken until cooked through (white in the center).

4. To assemble, stack chicken cutlet, tomato, and red onion on each gluten-free hamburger roll. Secure with toothpicks and cut in half. Serve with spicy mustard sauce.

Nutritional information: 339.5 calories, 26.9 grams of protein, 29.2 grams of carbohydrates, 11.4 grams of fat, 82.7 milligrams of cholesterol, 498.7 milligrams of sodium, 2.5 grams of fiber, 32.6 milligrams of calcium, 2.3 milligrams of iron

Allergen Notes and Additional Allergen Substitutions

- To make milk free, egg free, and soy free, omit the gluten-free hamburger rolls or check the rolls for each of these ingredients.

FODMAPs

- To make FODMAP friendly, substitute 1 tablespoon of garlic-infused oil (page 31) for the garlic and onion powders and omit the sliced onion. In the spicy mustard sauce, substitute maple syrup for the honey, substitute 1 tablespoon of water for the apple juice, and add an additional teaspoon of granulated sugar.

TIP: The spicy mustard is great on any sandwich or when thinned with water and served with a salad.

Sweets and Treats

I love sweets and although there are natural gluten-free options widely available, such as ice cream, pudding, and sorbet, I really crave moist cakes, flaky-crusted pies, buttery cookies, and other baked treats that traditionally contain gluten.

By experimenting with nut meals, fruit and nut butters, different types of sweeteners, butter, milk, and cooking techniques, I've turned my classic cravings into almond cherry tart, cannoli cones, black and white cookies, apple crumb pie, cream puffs, and rocky road.

These tried and true recipes will make anyone want to go gluten free, even if just for the day. Whip up some peach cobbler for a weeknight dessert, or chocolate covered macaroons for your next party, and bring my decadent chocolate peanut butter tart to your next potluck—I guarantee there won't be leftovers!

Chocolate Peanut Butter Tart

Aunt Louise and Eileen's Cheesecake

Black and White Cookies

Cannoli Cones

Peach Cobbler

Sweet Potato Pie

Cream Puffs

Apple Crumb Pie

Popcorn Balls

Cashew Butter Truffles

Almond Cherry Tart

Chocolate Covered Macaroons

Rocky Road

Pumpkin Tart with Bourbon Whipped Cream

Cinnamon Sugar Cookies

Double Peanut Butter Chocolate Chunk Cookies

Cherry Vanilla Chip Shortbread

Salted Carmel–Filled Fudge Cupcakes with Brown Sugar Frosting

Carrot Cake with Creamy Cream Cheese Frosting

Tres Leches Flan Cake

Chocolate Peanut Butter Tart   SERVES 22

GF, EF, FF, SFF, V

If you love chocolate and peanut butter (who doesn't?) you will love this decadently rich dessert. A very thin wedge is a true indulgence.

For the crust:

¾ cup almond meal

¾ cup gluten-free all-purpose flour blend

½ teaspoon xanthan gum

¼ teaspoon gluten-free baking powder

¼ teaspoon salt

½ cup granulated sugar

5 tablespoons light margarine, divided

3 to 4 tablespoons ice water

For the filling:

1½ cups of creamy peanut butter

⅓ cup powdered sugar

¼ cup coarsely chopped peanuts

2 teaspoons olive oil

1 (11.5-ounce) bag of gluten-free milk chocolate chips (or a combination of milk and dark chocolate chips)

1. Preheat oven to 400 degrees F.

2. Grease a 9-inch tart pan with 1 tablespoon margarine.

3. *To make crust:* Melt the remaining margarine in a small microwave-safe dish.

4. Mix together all dry ingredients for the crust, then slowly incorporate melted margarine. Add enough ice water so ingredients are moist enough to form a ball. Dough should not be too wet; it should only stick together if pressed together.

5. Press dough into the tart pan, covering bottom and sides completely and evenly.

6. Bake for about 12 minutes, until puffed and golden brown. Remove from oven.

7. *To make filling:* Microwave peanut butter until almost liquid, about 30 seconds. Stir in powdered sugar and spread evenly over crust. Sprinkle with chopped peanuts.

8. In a microwave-safe bowl, place oil and chocolate chips and microwave on high for one minute. Stir until well melted and creamy, with no solid pieces. Spread an even layer of chocolate over the top of the peanut butter.

9. Chill tart until chocolate is set, about 15 minutes, then remove from pan and leave at room temperature until ready to serve. Store at room temperature, covered, for up to a week.

Nutritional information: 264 calories, 6.3 grams of protein, 25.6 grams of carbohydrates, 17.2 grams of fat, 4.9 milligrams of cholesterol, 150 milligrams of sodium, 2.6 grams of fiber, 48 milligrams of calcium, <1 milligram of iron

Allergen Notes and Additional Allergen Substitutions

- To make vegan, use gluten-free vegan dark chocolate chips.

FODMAPs

- To make FODMAP friendly, substitute walnut meal for the almond meal.

TIPS: You can use ground gluten-free cereal, graham cracker crumbs, or ground nuts in place of the almond meal and gluten-free flour blend. An oversized spatula makes it easier to remove the bottom of the tart pan without disrupting the tart.

Aunt Louise and Eileen's Cheesecake

SERVES 21

GF, SF, NF, PF, FF, SFF, V

This is the ultimate cheesecake.

2 pounds cream cheese

1½ cups plus 1 tablespoon granulated sugar, divided

4 eggs

½ cup milk

2 cups sour cream

4 tablespoons cornstarch

1 tablespoon pure vanilla extract

1 tablespoon butter

1 pint of blueberries

1. Preheat oven to 370 degrees F.

2. Soften cream cheese in a deep bowl. Add 1½ cups sugar and mix well.

3. Add eggs one at a time, beating after each addition (best with an electric mixer). Add sour cream, milk, cornstarch, and vanilla. Mix after each addition.

4. Place a pan of water on the bottom rack in the oven; this will keep the cake from cracking.

5. Pour cream cheese mixture into either a 9-inch buttered springform pan or seven mini springform pans (each serves three) and bake for 20 minutes, until the top starts to brown lightly. Lower the temperature to 325 degrees F and continue to bake for one to one and one-quarter hours, until cheesecake holds firm when wiggled. Let the cheesecake cool, then unmold from the springform pan.

6. Serve cheesecake garnished with blueberries and a sprinkle of the remaining granulated sugar.

Nutritional information: 280 calories, 4.5 grams of protein, 19 grams of carbohydrates, 21 grams of fat, 94 milligrams of cholesterol, 198 milligrams of sodium, <1 gram of fiber, 76 milligrams of calcium, <1 milligram of iron

Allergen Notes and Additional Allergen Substitutions

- To make egg free, use a gluten-free, eggless egg substitute.

TIPS: Top with your favorite fruit, such as strawberries or blackberries, in place of blueberries. Will keep in the refrigerator for one week with topping and two weeks without.

Black and White Cookies

MAKES 12 LARGE OR 18 SMALL COOKIES
GF, SF, PF, FF, SFF, V

This sponge-like vanilla cookie iced on one side with chocolate glaze and the other side with vanilla glaze is a New York City classic. I couldn't find a gluten-free version I liked, so I needed to create my own!

For the cookie:

½ cup white rice flour

½ cup sorghum flour

¾ cup tapioca flour

¼ cup almond flour

1 teaspoon gluten-free baking powder

½ teaspoon sea salt

½ teaspoon xanthan gum

½ cup (8 tablespoons) unsalted butter, softened

¾ cup granulated sugar

1 egg

1 teaspoon pure vanilla extract

½ teaspoon lemon extract

½ cup buttermilk (or ½ cup whole milk mixed with ½ tablespoon of white vinegar)

¼ cup sparkling water

2 tablespoons water

For the icings:

2 tablespoons corn syrup

½ teaspoon pure vanilla extract

2 cups powdered sugar

1 ounce gluten-free unsweetened chocolate

1. Preheat oven to 375 degrees F. Line two baking sheets with parchment paper.

2. In a bowl, whisk together flours, baking powder, salt, and xanthan gum.

3. In a small bowl, combine buttermilk and sparkling water.

4. In a large mixing bowl, beat butter with an electric mixer for 30 seconds. Add sugar and beat until light and fluffy, about two minutes. Add egg, 1 teaspoon of vanilla extract, and the lemon extract. Beat together for about 30 seconds.

5. With mixer on low speed, alternately add flour mixture in four additions and buttermilk mixture in three additions, beginning and ending with flour. Mix until just combined.

6. Drop by ¼-cup (for large cookies) or 2-tablespoon scoops (for small cookies) onto prepared baking sheets. Bake for about 15 minutes, until set. Remove to a wire rack to cool.

7. *To make the icings:* Bring water and corn syrup to a boil in a medium saucepan. Remove from heat and whisk in vanilla and powdered sugar. Transfer ¾ cup of vanilla icing into a separate bowl.

8. Melt unsweetened chocolate in top of double boiler on the stove or in a microwave for 30-second increments. Add to ¾ cup of vanilla icing, mixing well.

9. Using a small offset spatula, spread vanilla icing onto a top half of each cookie. If the icing begins to thicken too much, add a teaspoon of warm water to thin. Allow to set for 15 minutes.

10. Again, using a small offset spatula, spread the chocolate icing on the other half of each cookie. If the chocolate icing gets too thick, add warm water, 1 teaspoon at a time, until it returns to a smoother, looser consistency. Allow the cookies to set for one hour at room temperature.

Nutritional information for 12 large cookies: 293 calories, 2.5 grams of protein, 48.5 grams of carbohydrates, 10.8 grams of fat, 36.2 milligrams of cholesterol, 124.5 milligrams of sodium, 1.2 grams of fiber, 80 milligrams of calcium, <1 milligram of iron

Nutritional information for 18 small cookies: 195 calories, 1.7 grams of protein, 32.4 grams of carbohydrates, 7.2 grams of fat, 24.1 milligrams of cholesterol, 83 milligrams of sodium, <1 gram of fiber, 53.3 milligrams of calcium, <1 milligram of iron

Allergen Notes and Additional Allergen Substitutions

- To make milk free, substitute margarine for the butter, substitute rice, coconut, or almond milk mixed with ½ tablespoon white vinegar for the buttermilk, and use dairy-free unsweetened chocolate.

- To make egg free, use a gluten-free, eggless egg substitute.

- To make nut free, omit the almond flour and add ¼ cup sorghum.

- To make vegan, substitute margarine for the butter, substitute rice, coconut, or almond milk mixed with ½ tablespoon white vinegar for the buttermilk, and use a gluten-free, vegan egg substitute and dairy-free unsweetened chocolate.

FODMAPs

- To make FODMAP friendly, substitute lactose-free, rice, or coconut milk mixed with ½ tablespoon white vinegar for the buttermilk and substitute maple syrup for the corn syrup.

TIPS: These cookies can be stored for up to three days in an airtight container. Keep in a single layer so the frosting doesn't smudge. They also freeze beautifully. Freeze on a baking sheet, individually wrap in plastic wrap, and store in a freezer bag. Let cookies defrost at room temperature.

 *Quick and easy*

Cannoli Cones SERVES 12

GF, EF*, NF*, PF, FF, SFF, V

Cannoli, an Italian pastry that originated in Sicily, are tube-shaped shells of fried pastry dough filled with a sweet, creamy filling that usually contains ricotta cheese. In this recipe, I use gluten-free ice cream cones to deliver my favorite part of this dessert—the rich, creamy filling dotted with chocolate chips. Gluten-free flours don't hold up as well in these types of shells, but gluten-free cones provide consistent quality, cut down on prep time, and substantially reduce the fat content.

- 1 pound whole milk ricotta cheese
- 1 cup powdered sugar
- 1 teaspoon pure vanilla extract
- 3 tablespoons mini semi-sweet chocolate chips
- 12 small gluten-free ice cream cones

1. Blend ricotta, powdered sugar, vanilla extract, and mini chocolate chips.
2. Use an ice cream scoop to fill cones and serve.

Nutritional iInformation: 124 calories, 4.3 grams of protein, 13.2 grams of carbohydrates, 5.7 grams of fat, 19.2 milligrams of cholesterol, 36.2 milligrams of sodium, <1 gram of fiber, 79.2 milligrams of calcium, <1 milligram of iron

Allergen Notes and Additional Allergen Substitutions

- To keep egg free and nut free, check the ice cream cones for eggs and nuts.
- To make soy free, check the cones for soy and use gluten-free, soy-free chocolate chips.

TIP: For chocolate filling, add cocoa powder to taste.

Peach Cobbler SERVES 6

GF, SF, PF, FF, SFF, V

Serve vanilla ice cream with these fresh sweet peaches topped with thick buttery crumbs.

4 cups fresh peaches, peeled and sliced

¾ cup sugar, divided

1½ teaspoons ground cinnamon, divided

½ cup white rice flour

⅓ cup tapioca flour

¼ cup almond flour

¼ teaspoon nutmeg

¼ cup light brown sugar

1 teaspoon gluten-free baking powder

¼ teaspoon salt

¼ teaspoon xanthan gum

1 egg

½ teaspoon almond extract

⅓ cup unsalted butter, melted

Powdered sugar, for dusting

1. Preheat oven to 350 degrees F.

2. Divide peaches among six individual ramekins. Combine ¼ cup sugar and ½ teaspoon cinnamon. Sprinkle over the peaches.

3. In a large bowl, combine flours, remaining cinnamon and sugar, nutmeg, brown sugar, baking powder, salt, xanthan gum, egg, and almond extract. With an electric mixer, beat at medium speed until mixture resembles coarse crumbs. Sprinkle over peaches.

4. Pour melted butter over topping. Bake 30 to 35 minutes, or until topping is lightly browned and peaches are tender.

5. Sprinkle with confectioner's sugar and serve warm.

Nutrition information: 354 calories, 3.9 grams of protein, 57 grams of carbohydrates, 13.2 grams of fat, 56.4 milligrams of cholesterol, 115 milligrams of sodium, 2.8 grams of fiber, 140 milligrams of calcium, <1 milligram of iron

Allergen Notes and Additional Allergen Substitutions

- To make milk free, substitute margarine for the butter.
- To make egg free, use a gluten-free, eggless egg substitute.
- To make nut free, substitute nut-free, gluten-free flour for the almond flour and vanilla extract for the almond extract.
- To make vegan, substitute margarine for the butter and use a gluten-free, vegan egg substitute.

FODMAPs

- To make FODMAP friendly, substitute papaya for the peaches and granulated white sugar for the brown sugar.

TIPS: To make one large cobbler, place peaches in a large casserole dish. If peaches are not in season, use frozen or canned and reduce cooking time.

Sweet Potato Pie   SERVES 8

GF, SF, PF, FF, SFF, V

A staple on many Thanksgiving tables, and an easy dessert to serve at any time. Pecans, coconut, and maple syrup add sweetness and crunch to the creamy filling.

For the pie crust:

1 cup white rice flour

½ cup tapioca flour

1 tablespoon powdered sugar

½ teaspoon sea salt

½ cup unsalted butter, cut into small pieces

4 to 6 tablespoons ice water

For the filling:

¼ cup unsalted butter, softened

¼ cup pure maple syrup

¼ cup granulated sugar

¼ cup pear puree

2 eggs

¾ cup fat-free evaporated milk

2 cups mashed sweet potatoes

1 teaspoon pure vanilla extract

1 teaspoon ground cinnamon

½ teaspoon ground nutmeg

¼ teaspoon sea salt

For the topping:

1 cup whole pecans

½ cup sweetened coconut

1 tablespoon pure maple syrup

1. Preheat oven to 425 degrees F.

2. *To make the crust:* Combine the flours, sugar, and salt in a large bowl.

3. Using a pastry blender, cut butter into flour mixture until it resembles coarse crumbs.

4. Add water, 1 tablespoon at a time, continuing to blend until all ingredients are moist.

5. Form dough into a ball and place on one sheet of waxed paper. Cover dough with a second sheet of waxed paper. Flatten dough with palm of hand, then roll out to a 10- to 11-inch circle that is ⅛-inch thick. Remove the top sheet and carefully invert into a 9-inch pie pan. Remove waxed paper. Gently press the dough down so it lines the bottom and sides of the pan. Trim excess dough.

6. *To make the filling:* In a large bowl, cream butter, maple syrup, sugar, and pear puree until soft and well combined. Add eggs and mix well.

7. Add milk, sweet potatoes, vanilla, cinnamon, nutmeg, and salt. Mix well until blended.

8. Pour filling into pie shell. Bake at 425 degrees F for 15 minutes. Reduce heat to 350 degrees F and bake an additional 35 to 40 minutes, until set. Cool for one hour.

9. *To make the topping:* Mix pecans and coconut with maple syrup. Spread on top of pie and broil for three to four minutes. Cool completely before serving.

Nutritional information, crust: 198.3 calories, 1.3 grams of protein, 21.8 grams of carbohydrates, 11.8 grams of fat, 30.5 milligrams of cholesterol, 147 milligrams of sodium, <1 gram of fiber, 5.4 milligrams of calcium, <1 milligram of iron

Nutritional information, filling: 360 calories, 4.8 grams of protein, 40 grams of carbohydrates, 20 grams of fat, 61 milligrams of cholesterol, 208 milligrams of sodium, 3.2 grams of fiber, 81.5 milligrams of cholesterol, <1 milligram of iron

Allergen Notes and Additional Allergen Substitutions

- To make milk free, substitute margarine for the butter and coconut milk for the evaporated milk.
- To make egg free, use a gluten-free, eggless egg substitute.

- To make nut free, omit the pecans.
- To make vegan, substitute margarine for the butter, substitute coconut milk for the evaporated milk, and use a gluten-free, vegan egg substitute.

FODMAPs
- To make FODMAP friendly, substitute crushed pineapple for the pear puree and ½ cup unsweetened lactose-free milk combined with ¼ cup heavy cream for the evaporated milk.

TIPS: Handle the dough carefully because it falls apart easily. Use excess dough to patch any tears. Top with a dollop of whipped cream instead of the pecan and coconut topping.

Cream Puffs   MAKES 18

GF, SF, NF, PF, FF, SFF, V

A light and airy puff of pastry filled with whipped cream! These pastry puffs are so versatile. Try filling them with pastry cream, pudding, or ice cream and drizzling with chocolate sauce for an even more indulgent treat. The tricks to these light pastry puffs are to keep stirring the flour blend into the butter until it forms together into a ball and to make sure the oven is at 400 degrees F when you bake them.

For the pastry:

1 cup water

½ cup unsalted butter

¾ cup white rice flour

¼ cup tapioca flour

½ teaspoon sea salt

¼ teaspoon xanthan gum

¼ teaspoon gluten-free baking powder

4 eggs

For the filling:

1 cup heavy whipping cream

3 tablespoons powdered sugar

1 teaspoon pure vanilla extract

1. Preheat oven to 400 degrees F. Line two baking sheets with parchment paper.

2. Combine the water and butter in a medium-size saucepan, heat until butter is melted, and bring to a boil.

3. In a large bowl, sift together rice flour, tapioca flour, salt, gum, and baking powder. Add to butter mixture and stir constantly until mixture rolls into a ball and leaves the side of the pan. This should take less than a minute. Remove from heat and cool for five minutes.

4. Add eggs, one at a time, beating well after each addition.

5. Drop by rounded tablespoons onto prepared baking sheets. Bake for 20 to 25 minutes, until light golden brown. Remove from oven and cool.

6. *To make filling:* Pour the cream and vanilla into a mixing bowl and begin to whip on high speed. Gradually sprinkle in 2 tablespoons of sugar as the cream whips. Whip until stiff, but be careful not to over whip.

7. Cut tops off cream puffs. Fill bottom with cream, then replace tops. Sprinkle with remaining 1 tablespoon powdered sugar and serve.

Nutrition information: 141 calories, 2.1 grams of protein, 8 grams of carbohydrates, 11.2 grams of fat, 73 milligrams of cholesterol, 87 milligrams of sodium, <1 gram of fiber, 26.8 milligrams of calcium, <1 gram of fiber

Allergen Notes and Additional Allergen Substitutions

- To make milk free, substitute margarine for the butter and a dairy-free whipped cream for the filling.
- To make egg free, use a gluten-free, eggless egg substitute.
- To make vegan, substitute margarine for the butter, substitute a dairy-free whipped cream for the filling, and use a gluten-free, vegan egg substitute.

TIPS: Flavor the whipped cream with any pure extract such as lemon, almond, or orange. Sprinkle in some cocoa powder with the sugar to make chocolate whipped cream. The unfilled puffs freeze beautifully in a freezer bag.

Apple Crumb Pie   SERVES 10

GF, EF, SF, PF, FF, SFF, V

I can't make up my mind which I like better: light apple pastry or apple crumb pie. This recipe gives me the best of both. What could be better than luscious apple pie nestled under a buttery brown sugar topping?

For the crust:

See pie crust recipe on page 138

For the filling:

6 cups apples (about 8 if small or 4 to 5 if large), such as Macintosh or Granny Smith, peeled and thinly sliced

½ cup granulated sugar

2 tablespoons white rice flour

¾ teaspoon ground cinnamon

⅛ teaspoon ground nutmeg

For the crumbs:

¼ cup white rice flour

¼ cup almond flour

¼ cup packed brown sugar

¼ teaspoon ground cinnamon

¼ cup unsalted butter, softened

1. Heat oven to 375 degrees F.

2. *To make the filling:* Mix apples, sugar, rice flour, cinnamon, and nutmeg in a large bowl.

3. *To make the crumbs:* In a separate bowl, add rice flour, almond flour, brown sugar, and cinnamon. Cut in butter with a pastry blender until mixture resembles coarse crumbs.

4. To assemble, place apples in prepared pie crust. Sprinkle crumbs evenly over top. Bake for 40 to 45 minutes, until apples are tender and topping is browned.

Nutritional information: 328 calories, 2.9 grams of protein, 45.5 grams of carbohydrates, 15.6 grams of fat, 36.6 milligrams of cholesterol, 119.9 milligrams of sodium, 2.72 grams of fiber, 21 milligrams of calcium, <1 milligram of iron

Allergen Notes and Additional Allergen Substitutions

- To make milk free and vegan, substitute margarine for the butter.
- To make nut free, substitute gluten-free all-purpose flour blend for the almond flour.

TIP: Add a few tablespoons of walnuts and raisins or dried cranberries to the filling for a yummy twist.

 *Quick and easy*

Popcorn Balls MAKES 12

GF, EF, SF, NF, FF, SFF, V

A sticky, chewy, holiday treat for kids of all ages! Personalize these by mixing in nuts, chocolate chips, mini M & Ms, or marshmallows.

12 cups plain popped popcorn

1 cup granulated sugar

½ cup light corn syrup

2 tablespoons unsalted butter

½ teaspoon sea salt

1 teaspoon pure vanilla extract

⅓ cup salted peanuts (optional)

1. Place popcorn in a large roasting pan or bowl.

2. Combine sugar, corn syrup, butter, and salt in a heavy 2-quart saucepan. Stirring constantly, bring to a boil over medium heat. Boil rapidly for two minutes. Remove from heat. Stir in vanilla and peanuts, if using.

3. Pour syrup mixture over popcorn, stirring to coat well. Cover hands with two plastic sandwich bags. Working quickly, shape into twelve 3-inch popcorn balls.

4. Place on parchment or waxed paper to cool completely.

Nutritional information: 179.4 calories, 2.1 grams of protein, 34 grams of carbohydrates, 4.3 grams of fat, 5 milligrams of cholesterol, 119.7 milligrams of sodium, 1.1 grams of fiber, 3.3 milligrams of calcium, <1 milligram of iron

Allergen Notes and Additional Allergen Substitutions

- To make milk free and vegan, substitute margarine for the butter.
- To make peanut free, omit the peanuts.

FODMAP Friendly

TIP: Make these more festive by adding colorful gluten-free candy (such as mini M&Ms) to the popcorn before pouring on the syrup.

 *Quick and easy*

Cashew Butter Truffles   MAKES 24

GF, EF, SF*, PF, FF, SFF, V

Cashew butter and chocolate is one of my favorite flavor combinations. Granola and coconut add a wonderful crunch to these decadent, bite-size truffles.

½ cup creamy cashew butter

½ cup unsalted butter

1 teaspoon vanilla extract

2 cups confectioner's sugar

½ cup gluten-free granola, crushed

½ cup toasted, gluten-free sweetened coconut

1. In a microwave-safe bowl, place cashew butter and butter. Microwave on low until melted, about one minute.

2. Stir in vanilla and sugar.

3. Form into twenty-four 1-inch balls. Roll half of the truffles in granola and the other half in coconut.

4. Place on a cookie sheet lined with parchment paper and refrigerate for at least one hour.

Nutritional information: 119 calories, 1.4 grams of protein, 12 grams of carbohydrates, 7.8 grams of fat, 10 milligrams of cholesterol, 39 milligrams of sodium, <1 gram of fiber, 5.8 milligrams of calcium, <1 milligram of iron

Allergen Notes and Additional Allergen Substitutions

- To keep soy free, check the granola for soy.
- To keep nut free, check the granola for nuts.
- To make milk free and vegan, substitute margarine for the butter and omit the granola (unless the granola is dairy free).

TIPS: You can also use almond or peanut butter and almond extract in place of the cashew butter and vanilla extract. Roll in any toppings you like, sprinkle with powdered sugar, or leave plain.

Almond Cherry Tart   SERVES 14

GF, SF*, PF, FF, SFF, V

This tart is truly a showstopper and worth the time it takes to make it. A flaky, French pastry–like crust cradles layers of almond cream and tart cherries. A burst of flavor in every bite!

For the crust:

9 tablespoons salted butter, softened, divided

1 egg yolk

1¼ cups gluten-free all-purpose flour blend

¾ cup almond meal

2 tablespoons granulated sugar

1 teaspoon xanthan gum

For the filling:

1 pound (about 3 to 4 cups) fresh cherries, pitted

2 tablespoons brandy (optional)

8 tablespoons granulated sugar, divided

3 tablespoons salted butter

1 egg

1 teaspoon pure vanilla extract

½ cup almond meal

1 tablespoon gluten-free all-purpose flour blend

3 tablespoons raspberry preserves

2 tablespoons confectioner's sugar (optional)

1. Preheat oven to 350 degrees F.

2. *To make the crust:* Cream 8 tablespoons of butter and egg yolk together.

3. In a separate bowl, mix all dry ingredients together.

4. Combine dry ingredients with creamed mixture until you are able to form dough into a ball. The dough should be able to hold together without being too sticky. Add extra flour if too wet.

5. Wrap in plastic wrap and put in the freezer for 10 minutes.

6. Rub 1 tablespoon butter on a tart pan.

7. Press dough into bottom and sides of tart pan.

8. Bake tart shell for 8 to 10 minutes, until just turning golden.

9. *To make the filling:* In a bowl, mix together pitted cherries, brandy (if desired), and 3 tablespoons of sugar. Set aside.

10. In a large bowl, whip butter until fluffy. Add 4 tablespoons of sugar and beat until light and creamy.

11. Add egg and vanilla and beat for three minutes, until fluffy.

12. Add almond meal and flour and beat for one to two minutes.

13. To assemble, pour almond cream into crust. Evenly distribute.

14. With a slotted spoon, separate cherries from liquid and arrange on top of the almond cream. Reserve remaining liquid.

15. Bake for 30 minutes, or until almond cream is puffed and starting to turn golden.

16. Meanwhile, in a small saucepan over medium heat, bring remaining cherry liquid, 1 tablespoon of sugar, and raspberry preserves to a boil; lower heat, and simmer until it thickens a bit.

17. When tart is done, brush raspberry mixture on each cherry to glaze top of tart.

18. When cooled, carefully remove tart from the pan and serve.

19. Garnish with powdered sugar if so desired.

Nutritional information: 262 calories, 3.7 grams of protein, 28 grams of carbohydrates, 15.6 grams of fat, 52 milligrams of cholesterol, 91.1 milligrams of sodium, 1.7 grams of fiber, 42.4 milligrams of calcium, <1 milligram of iron

Allergen Notes and Additional Allergen Substitutions

- To keep soy free, check the gluten-free all-purpose flour blend for soy.
- To make milk free, substitute margarine for the butter.
- To make egg free, use a gluten-free, eggless egg substitute.

- To make nut free, substitute a gluten-free all-purpose flour blend for the almond meal.
- To make vegan, substitute margarine for the butter and use a gluten-free, vegan egg substitute.

TIP: You can pit cherries with a paring knife, but a cherry pitter, available at gourmet stores, makes it much easier.

Chocolate Covered Macaroons   SERVES 18

GF, PF, FF, SFF, V

These chewy coconut macaroons covered in a thick layer of chocolate will keep for weeks in a sealed cookie tin.

1⅓ cups sweetened coconut

⅓ cup granulated sugar

3 tablespoons brown rice flour

½ teaspoon salt

2 egg whites

½ teaspoon almond extract

Gluten-free cooking spray

¾ cup gluten-free chocolate chips (semisweet or milk chocolate)

1. Preheat oven to 325 degrees F.

2. Mix together coconut, sugar, brown rice flour, salt, egg whites, and almond extract until well combined. If too wet to scoop, add a little more rice flour.

3. Spray a baking sheet with cooking spray.

4. Drop the batter onto baking sheet using a 1-tablespoon cookie scoop.

5. Bake for about 10 minutes, until golden, taking care not to burn the bottom of the cookies.

6. Remove macaroons from baking sheet with a spatula and place on aluminum foil to cool.

7. Meanwhile, place chocolate chips in a small microwave-safe bowl, microwave on low for one minute, and stir. Continue to microwave in 15-second intervals, stirring regularly, until chocolate is melted and smooth.

8. Dip tops of macaroons into the chocolate mixture, rotating to coat completely.

9. Place macaroons back on the aluminum foil and let cool one or more hours, until chocolate is hard.

10. Store in an airtight container until ready to serve.

Nutritional information: 69.4 calories, 1.1 grams of protein, 9.3 grams of carbohydrates, 3.3 grams of fat, 4 milligrams of cholesterol, 94.6 milligrams of sodium, <1 gram of fiber, <1 milligram of calcium, <1 milligram of iron

Allergen Notes and Additional Allergen Substitutions

- To make milk free, use dairy-free chocolate chips or omit them.
- To make egg free, use a gluten-free, eggless egg substitute.
- To make soy free, use soy-free cooking spray and soy-free chocolate chips (or omit them).
- To make nut free, substitute vanilla extract for the almond extract.
- To make vegan, use a gluten-free, vegan egg substitute and dairy-free chocolate chips (or omit them).

TIP: Instead of dipping in chocolate, dollop each macaroon with ½ teaspoon of your favorite jam before baking.

 *Quick and easy*

Rocky Road SERVES 20

GF, EF, FF, SFF, V

This combination of chocolate, marshmallows, and nuts provides a medley of textures and flavors in each bite: sweet, salty, crunchy, and soft. Get creative with other mix-ins. I also like gluten-free pretzels and crushed potato chips.

1 (11.5-ounce) bag gluten-free dark chocolate chips

1 cup mini marshmallows

1 cup whole walnuts

½ cup peanuts

1. Place chocolate chips in a small microwave-safe bowl, microwave on low for one minute, and stir. Continue to microwave in 15-second intervals, stirring regularly, until chocolate is melted and smooth.

2. Cover a baking sheet with waxed paper.

3. Mix half the marshmallows and nuts with melted chocolate.

4. Pour mixture over waxed paper and top with remaining marshmallows and nuts. If you like sweet and salty, sprinkle with a pinch of sea salt.

5. Put in refrigerator until firm, about 10 minutes.

6. Break into large chunks with a knife, and serve.

Nutritional information: 156.7 calories, 2.6 grams of protein, 13.2 grams of carbohydrates, 10.8 grams of fat, 1.1 milligrams of cholesterol, 5.9 milligrams of sodium, 1.8 grams of fiber, 16.9 milligrams of calcium, 1.5 milligrams of iron

Allergen Notes and Additional Allergen Substitutions

- To make milk free and vegan, use dairy-free chocolate chips.
- To make soy free, use soy-free chocolate chips.

TIP: Any kind of nut can be used in this recipe. If you like salty with your sweet, use salted nuts.

Pumpkin Tart with Bourbon Whipped Cream SERVES 12

GF, SF*, PF*, FF, SFF, V

Tarts are sure to impress and gluten-free tarts are easy to make because the gluten-free dough doesn't fight you when you try to roll it. I love this one so much I often make an extra tart, cut it into slices, and freeze the slices for individual servings whenever I need them.

For the crust:

¾ cup almond meal

1 cup gluten-free all-purpose flour blend

4 tablespoons salted butter, melted, plus 1 tablespoon

4 tablespoons granulated sugar

1 teaspoon pure vanilla extract

½ teaspoon gluten-free baking powder

½ teaspoon sea salt

2 to 3 tablespoons ice water

For the filling:

¾ cup granulated sugar

½ teaspoon sea salt

1½ teaspoons ground cinnamon

½ teaspoon allspice or pumpkin pie spice

Dash of nutmeg

2 eggs

1 (15-ounce) can pumpkin puree

1 (12-ounce) can 2% evaporated milk

For the bourbon whipped cream:

1 pint heavy cream

1 teaspoon pure vanilla extract

½ cup powdered sugar

1 tablespoon bourbon

1. Preheat oven to 350 degrees F.

2. *To make crust:* Use a fork to combine almond meal, gluten-free flour blend, and melted butter until crumbly.

3. Add sugar, vanilla, baking powder, and sea salt and combine. Add just enough ice water until you can work dough into a ball.

4. Wrap dough ball in plastic wrap and place in the freezer for 10 to 15 minutes.

5. Rub remaining butter into a 10-inch tart pan.

6. On a piece of waxed paper, sprinkle a little gluten-free flour blend and place dough on the waxed paper. Roll out, adding more flour blend if needed, until it is a little larger than the tart pan. Flip dough into tart pan and try to distribute evenly. If the dough cracks or breaks, just push dough into the pan and smooth out, making sure to completely cover the sides as well.

7. Bake tart shell for 10 to 15 minutes, until starting to brown and puff.

8. *To make filling:* Preheat oven to 400 degrees F.

9. In a large bowl, combine sugar, salt, spices, and eggs.

10. Blend in pumpkin until creamy, and then incorporate evaporated milk.

11. Pour into prepared tart shell.

12. Bake for 15 minutes, then lower temperature to 350 degrees F and bake for 45 minutes, or until a toothpick in center comes out clean.

13. Cool at room temperature for one and one-half hours, then refrigerate until ready to serve.

14. *To make the bourbon whipped cream:* Whip heavy cream until soft peaks begin to form. While beating, add vanilla extract and powdered sugar, a little at a time, until just combined. Add bourbon and whip until stiff peaks form. Be careful not to overbeat or the cream will become lumpy and butter-like. Refrigerate until ready to serve with tart.

Nutritional information, pie and crust: 207.4 calories, 5.6 grams of protein, 25.2 grams of carbohydrates, 9.7 grams of fat, 48.7 milligrams of cholesterol, 270.2 milligrams of sodium, 2.1 grams of fiber, 139.2 milligrams of calcium, 1.1 milligrams of iron

Nutritional information, bourbon whipped cream: 155.2 calories, <1 gram of protein, 5.3 grams of carbohydrates, 14.8 grams of fat, 54.8 milligrams of cholesterol, 15.3 milligrams of sodium, 0 grams of fiber, 26 milligrams of calcium, <1 milligram of iron

Allergen Notes and Additional Allergen Substitutions

- To keep soy free and peanut free, check the gluten-free all-purpose flour blend for soy and peanuts.
- To make milk free, substitute vegetable oil or margarine for the butter, coconut milk for the evaporated milk, and a dairy-free milk for the heavy cream. Or use another milk-free whipped topping.
- To make nut free, check the gluten-free all-purpose flour blend for nuts and substitute gluten-free all-purpose flour blend for the almond meal.
- To make egg free, use a gluten-free, eggless egg substitute.
- To make vegan, substitute vegetable oil or margarine for the butter, coconut milk for the evaporated milk, and a dairy-free milk for the heavy cream; or use another milk-free whipped topping. Use a gluten-free, vegan egg substitute.

FODMAP Friendly

TIP: Use this crust for a savory tart by omitting the sugar and substituting bean flours (such as chickpea) for the almond meal.

Cinnamon Sugar Cookies   MAKES 2 DOZEN

GF, NF, PF, FF, SFF, V

Lightly spiced with a kick of cinnamon, these cookies remind me of the Snickerdoodles I tasted in Pennsylvania Dutch Country.

⅓ cup unsalted butter

2 tablespoons ground flaxseed

1 cup granulated sugar, divided

½ cup packed light brown sugar

1 egg

1 teaspoon pure vanilla extract

1¼ cups white rice flour

¾ cup tapioca flour

½ teaspoon xanthan gum

½ teaspoon baking soda

½ teaspoon gluten-free baking powder

1½ teaspoons ground cinnamon, divided

¼ teaspoon ground cloves

¼ teaspoon ground nutmeg

¼ teaspoon ground ginger

2 tablespoons coconut milk

1 cup Hershey's cinnamon chips

1. Preheat oven to 350 degrees F. Line baking pans with parchment paper.

2. Beat butter, flaxseed, ½ cup granulated sugar, brown sugar, egg, and vanilla in a large bowl until light and creamy.

3. In a separate bowl, sift together rice flour, tapioca flour, xanthan gum, baking soda, baking powder, ½ teaspoon cinnamon, cloves, nutmeg, and ginger.

4. Add half of flour mixture to butter mixture and beat well. Add coconut milk and beat until well blended. Stir in cinnamon chips.

5. In a small bowl, combine remaining sugar and cinnamon.

6. Form cookies into 2-inch balls. Roll in cinnamon sugar and place on prepared baking pans. Bake for 8 to 10 minutes, until bottoms of cookies are lightly browned. Remove from baking sheets and place on a wire rack to cool completely.

Nutrition information: 161.7 calories, 1.6 grams of protein, 24.9 grams of carbohydrates, 5.9 grams of fat, 14.1 milligrams of cholesterol, 62 milligrams of sodium, <1 gram of fiber, 23.3 milligrams of calcium, <1 milligram of iron

Allergen Notes and Additional Allergen Substitutions

- To make milk free, substitute margarine for the butter and check the cinnamon chips for milk.

- To make egg free, use a gluten-free, eggless egg substitute.

- To make soy free, use homemade cinnamon chips (see tip for recipe).

- To make vegan, substitute margarine for the butter, use a gluten-free, vegan egg substitute, and use homemade cinnamon chips (see tip for recipe).

FODMAPs

- To make FODMAP friendly, substitute granulated sugar for the light brown sugar, and use homemade cinnamon chips (see tip for recipe).

TIP: Make your own cinnamon chips by combining ⅔ cup sugar, 2 tablespoons soft butter, 3 tablespoons cinnamon, 3 tablespoons corn syrup, and ¼ teaspoon vanilla. Spread on a cookie sheet and bake in a 300 degree F oven for about 15 to 20 minutes, until bubbly. Cool completely, then chop into small pieces.

Double Peanut Butter Chocolate Chunk Cookies MAKES 3 DOZEN

GF, FF, SFF, V

These chewy on the inside and crispy on the outside cookies are bursting with chunks of chocolate and creamy peanut butter. If you leave them out they won't last long!

½ cup granulated sugar

½ cup packed brown sugar

½ cup creamy peanut butter

½ cup unsalted butter, softened

1 egg

1 teaspoon pure vanilla extract

¾ cup white rice flour

½ cup tapioca flour

½ teaspoon xanthan gum

¾ teaspoon baking soda

½ teaspoon baking powder

¼ teaspoon salt

6 gluten-free peanut butter cups, roughly chopped (do not use seasonal shaped items without checking gluten-free status)

1. Cream together sugars, peanut butter, butter, egg, and vanilla in a large bowl until well combined.

2. In a separate bowl, sift together rice flour, tapioca flour, xanthan gum, baking soda, baking powder, and salt. Stir into peanut butter mixture. Mix in peanut butter cups.

3. Form into a long round log (about 12 inches long and 2 inches around). Wrap in plastic wrap and place in refrigerator for at least two hours.

4. Preheat oven to 375 degrees F. Line a baking sheet with parchment paper.

5. Remove cookie dough from refrigerator. Slice into ¼-inch-thick slices and place on baking sheet. Bake for 8 to 10 minutes, until lightly browned. Remove from baking sheet and place on a wire rack to cool.

Nutritional information: 99 calories, 1.5 grams of protein, 11.3 grams of carbohydrates, 5.5 grams of fat, 12.3 milligrams of cholesterol, 75 milligrams of sodium, <1 gram of fiber, 14.9 milligrams of calcium, <1 milligram of iron

Allergen Notes and Additional Allergen Substitutions

• To make egg free, use a gluten-free, eggless egg substitute.

TIP: Reese's peanut butter cups are currently listed as gluten free on the Hershey's website. However, recipes may change, so always confirm that an item is gluten free before using.

Cherry Vanilla Chip Shortbread   SERVES 12

GF*, EF, NF, PF, FF, SFF, V

Delicate and buttery, these melt in your mouth. Perfect with a cup of tea.

Gluten-free cooking spray

½ cup (8 tablespoons) unsalted butter, softened

½ cup powdered sugar

1 teaspoon pure vanilla extract

½ cup white rice flour

¼ cup tapioca flour

¼ cup cornmeal

⅛ teaspoon sea salt

⅓ cup dried cherries

¼ cup Hershey's Premier White Chips

1. Preheat oven to 350 degrees F. Spray a 9-inch cake pan with cooking spray and line with parchment paper.

2. In a large mixing bowl, beat butter and sugar until smooth and creamy. Add vanilla.

3. In a separate bowl, sift flours, cornmeal, and salt together. Add to butter mixture and beat until well incorporated.

4. Stir in cherries and white chips. Press dough into prepared pan. Smooth top with fingers or small rolling pin. Prick the dough in several places with a fork to allow steam to escape while baking.

5. Bake for 35 to 40 minutes, until light golden brown on top and deeper brown around the edges.

6. Remove from oven and immediately turn out onto a clean work surface. Remove parchment paper. Cut into 12 pieces using a sharp knife or pizza cutter. Transfer to a wire rack to cool.

Nutritional information: 163.1 calories, <1 gram of protein, 20.3 grams of carbohydrates, 9.1 grams of fat, 20.3 milligrams of cholesterol, 38 milligrams of sodium, <1 gram of fiber, 5.4 milligrams of calcium, <1 milligram of iron

Allergen Notes and Additional Allergen Substitutions

- To keep gluten free, confirm Hershey's Premier White baking chips are still gluten free. They are at the time of this writing.

TIP: This dough can be rolled out on a floured surface until ½-inch thick, and cut by hand or cookie cutter. Place on a greased baking sheet and bake for 14 to 16 minutes.

Salted Caramel–Filled Fudge Cupcakes with Brown Sugar Frosting SERVES 20

GF, NF, PF, FF, SFF, V

A decadent chocolate cupcake with a fudge-like consistency and gooey caramel filling. These cupcakes are perfect for a birthday party, and unfrosted cupcakes freeze beautifully.

For the cupcakes:

¾ cup dark chocolate chips

¼ cup unsweetened cocoa powder

1 cup unsalted butter

¾ cup white rice flour

¼ cup tapioca flour

½ teaspoon gluten-free baking powder

¼ teaspoon sea salt

¼ teaspoon xanthan gum

½ cup brown sugar

1 cup granulated sugar

4 eggs

1 teaspoon pure vanilla extract

For the filling:

1 cup granulated sugar

½ cup heavy cream

2 tablespoons unsalted butter

1 teaspoon coarse sea salt

For the frosting:

½ cup unsalted butter

1 cup brown sugar

¼ cup milk

2 cups powdered sugar

1. Preheat oven to 325 degrees F. Line 20 muffin cups with paper liners.

2. *To make cupcakes:* Place chocolate chips, cocoa powder, and butter in top of a double boiler. Heat, stirring occasionally, until mixture is melted and smooth. Remove from heat and allow to cool to lukewarm.

3. In a large bowl, whisk together flours, baking powder, salt, xanthan gum, and sugars. Beat in eggs, one at a time. Stir in the chocolate mixture and vanilla.

4. Scoop into muffin cups, filling ¾ full. Bake for 20 to 25 minutes, until cakes spring back when pressed on. Remove from oven and set aside to cool.

5. *To make salted caramel filling:* Heat 1 cup sugar in a small saucepan over medium heat. Cook, stirring constantly, until the sugar has melted and turns a deep amber color. Remove from heat and slowly whisk in cream. Whisk in butter and salt. Transfer to a dish to cool.

6. *To make frosting:* Melt butter and brown sugar in a small saucepan. Boil for two minutes, stirring constantly. Add milk. Continue to stir until mixture boils again. Remove from heat and cool.

7. In a large bowl, beat powdered sugar into brown sugar mixture a little at a time.

8. To assemble, remove a small portion from the top of the cupcake using a melon scoop. Pour 1 teaspoon caramel sauce into cupcake and replace top. Pipe frosting using a pastry bag or spread frosting on top of cupcake.

Nutritional information: 349 calories, 1.5 grams of protein, 46.7 grams of carbohydrates, 18.7 grams of fat, 80 milligrams of cholesterol, 60 milligrams of sodium, <1 gram of fiber, 27.5 milligrams of calcium, <1 milligram of iron

TIP: Save a step by using prepared gluten-free caramel sauce.

Carrot Cake with Creamy Cream Cheese Frosting   SERVES 16

GF, PF*, FF, SFF, V

This moist cake is packed with carrots, raisins, and walnuts and topped with my favorite cream cheese frosting.

For the cake:

Gluten-free cooking spray

½ cup brown rice flour

¼ cup tapioca flour

¼ cup almond flour

1 teaspoon gluten-free baking powder

½ teaspoon baking soda

1 teaspoon ground cinnamon

½ teaspoon xanthan gum

¼ teaspoon sea salt

½ cup granulated sugar

½ cup brown sugar

¼ cup canola oil

1 tablespoon ground flaxseed

1 egg

1 egg white

1 teaspoon pure vanilla extract

½ cup crushed pineapple, drained

¾ cup finely grated carrots

¼ cup golden raisins

¼ cup chopped walnuts

For the cream cheese frosting:

    1 (8-ounce) package light cream cheese

    4 cups powdered sugar

    2 tablespoons unsalted butter, softened

    1 teaspoon pure vanilla extract

1. Preheat oven to 350 degrees F. Spray a 9-inch square baking pan with cooking spray.

2. *To make the cake:* In a large bowl, sift together flours, baking powder, baking soda, cinnamon, xanthan gum, and salt.

3. In another large bowl, beat sugars, oil, and flaxseed (if using), until well blended. Add egg, egg white, and vanilla. Continue mixing until well combined.

4. Stir flour mixture into wet ingredients until just combined. Do not overmix.

5. Fold in pineapple, carrots, raisins, and walnuts. Pour batter into prepared pan.

6. Bake for 30 to 35 minutes, or until toothpick inserted into cake comes out clean. Remove from oven and let cool.

7. *To make the frosting:* Beat together cream cheese, sugar, butter, and vanilla until smooth and creamy.

8. Cover cooled cake with frosting and serve.

Nutritional information: 290 calories, 4.2 grams of protein, 43.5 grams of carbohydrates, 11.9 grams of fat, 34 milligrams of cholesterol, 176 milligrams of sodium, <1 gram of fiber, 49 milligrams of calcium, <1 milligram of iron

Allergen Notes and Additional Allergen Substitutions

- To keep peanut free, check the almond meal for peanuts.
- To make egg free, use a gluten-free, eggless egg substitute.
- To make soy free, use soy-free cooking spray.

FODMAPs

- To make FODMAP friendly, substitute granulated sugar for brown sugar, omit the raisins, and sprinkle the cake with powdered sugar instead of frosting.

TIPS: Sprinkle with finely ground walnuts before serving. This recipe easily doubles.

Tres Leches Flan Cake   SERVES 14

GF, NF*, PF, FF, SFF, V

I have always loved tres leches cake: a layer of moist yellow cake with a hint of citrus, topped with creamy custard and caramel. Using yellow cake mix makes my version easier to prepare without losing any of the flavor of the classic recipe.

Gluten-free cooking spray

1 box (single cake size) gluten-free yellow cake mix

1 cup orange flavored seltzer

2 teaspoons grated orange zest, divided

14 ounces sweetened condensed milk

12 ounces fat-free evaporated milk

3 eggs

1 tablespoon pure vanilla extract

1 cup granulated sugar

1. Preheat oven to 350 degrees F. Spray a 9-inch springform pan with cooking spray. Cover the bottom and sides with aluminum foil.

2. In a mixing bowl, beat cake mix with seltzer and 1 teaspoon orange zest until smooth and well blended. Set aside.

3. In a blender, mix remaining orange zest with condensed milk, evaporated milk, eggs, and vanilla until well blended. Set aside.

4. Pour the sugar into a skillet and cook on medium-high heat. Continue cooking and stirring until the sugar dissolves and it turns golden brown. Do not overcook.

5. Pour the caramel into the bottom of the prepared springform pan. Top with the cake batter. Gently pour the flan down the sides of pan.

6. Place in oven and cook for 45 minutes, or until set.

7. Remove from oven. Let cool then refrigerate for several hours or overnight. Invert onto serving dish. Remove outer ring of pan. Let cake sit on plate while warming to room temperature. Remove bottom of pan, leaving a layer of caramel on top.

Nutrition information: 316 calories, 6.8 grams of protein, 64 grams of carbohydrates, 4.3 grams of fat, 55 milligrams of cholesterol, 266 milligrams of sodium, <1 gram of fiber, 172 milligrams of calcium, <1 gram fiber

Allergen Notes and Additional Allergen Substitutions

- To keep nut free, check the cake mix for nuts.

TIP: Be sure to let the cake cool completely before taking it out of the pan. This flan topping is firm on the cake and will not be runny when you serve it.

Cooking for a Crowd

W hen it comes to entertaining, the best choices are those that reheat well or hold up well over a sterno. When I'm hosting a party, I find it best to offer all gluten-free options on the buffet or to set up a separate table for the gluten-free food to prevent cross-contamination by impatient guests who may use the wrong spoon to serve themselves.

Rosemarie's Pasta with Sun-Dried Tomatoes and Sausage Bolognese

Holiday Ham with Pineapple Glaze

Brisket with Cranberry-Chili Glaze

Stir-Fried Rice Noodles with Peanuts

Lemon Chicken

Linguini with Shrimp and Petite Diced Tomatoes

Hawaiian Chicken

Chicken with Mushrooms and Cream Sauce

Macaroni and Cheese
Braised Short Ribs
Turkey Meat Loaf
Oven-Baked "Fried" Chicken

Rosemarie's Pasta with Sun-Dried Tomatoes and Sausage Bolognese   SERVES 8

GF, SF*, PF, FF, SFF

This is one of my sister-in-law Rosemarie's signature dishes. Sun-dried tomatoes add a burst of flavor and a new twist on this Italian classic.

  1 pound cooked gluten-free rigatoni

  2 tablespoons olive oil

  ½ small onion, diced

  2 cloves garlic, chopped

  3 large links (4 ounces each) gluten-free cheese and parsley sausage, removed from their casings

  6 to 8 sun-dried tomatoes (not in oil), diced

  ½ cup red wine

  3 tablespoons pesto sauce, store bought or recipe (page 171)

  1 quart (32 ounces) no salt added tomato sauce

  2 tablespoons Parmesan cheese

1. In a large skillet over medium-high heat, sauté onion in olive oil until translucent, then add garlic.

2. Break up sausage with a fork and add to skillet. Stir occasionally until lightly browned. Add sun-dried tomatoes and stir.

3. Add remaining ingredients except the pasta and simmer about 20 minutes, until flavors blend.

4. Check seasonings and add more garlic or pesto if desired.

5. Pour over cooked rigatoni and serve with Parmesan cheese.

Nutritional information: 384.8 calories, 13.1 grams of protein, 57 grams of carbohydrates, 11.9 grams of fat, 36 milligrams of cholesterol, 409 milligrams of sodium, 7.7 grams of fiber, 70 milligrams of calcium, 1.7 milligrams of iron

Allergen Notes and Additional Allergen Substitutions

- To keep soy free, check the pasta and store-bought pesto sauce pasta for soy.

TIP: Serve over gluten-free spaghetti or spaghetti squash.

 *Quick and easy*

Homemade Pesto   SERVES 48

GF, EF, SF, PF, FF, SFF, V

This fragrant pesto from my sister-in-law Rosemarie holds up well in the refrigerator or the freezer. Serve it hot or cold over vegetables, pasta, meat, or fish, or add to pizza.

- 4 cups packed basil leaves
- ¾ cup grated Romano cheese
- 8 cloves garlic
- ⅓ cup pine nuts
- Handful of parsley
- 1 teaspoon salt
- 1 cup olive oil
- Splash of lemon juice

1. Puree basil, cheese, garlic, nuts, parsley, and salt in a food processor.
2. While food processor is running, slowly drizzle in olive oil and then lemon juice. Process until smooth or the consistency you prefer.

Nutritional information: 51 calories, .7 grams of protein, <1 gram of carbohydrates, 5.5 grams of fat, 1.1 milligrams of cholesterol, 68 milligrams of sodium, <1 gram of fiber, 20 milligrams of calcium, 20 milligrams of iron

FODMAPs
- To make FODMAP friendly, omit the garlic cloves and substitute garlic-infused oil (page 31) for the olive oil.

TIPS: Pesto can be made with other nuts such as walnuts, almonds, or pecans, and Parmesan cheese can be used in place of the Romano cheese. Replace olive oil with a flavored oil for extra depth. Use your imagination! Before storing in the freezer, top sauce with a dash of lemon juice and olive oil.

Holiday Ham with Pineapple Glaze

SERVES 16

GF*, MF, EF, SF, NF, PF, FF, SFF

This dish is a perfect centerpiece for an Easter holiday dinner. Many store-bought hams with flavoring packets have gluten added to them. This recipe gives you all of the flavor you are looking for with simple, easy to find ingredients. I use ginger ale instead of cola because it gives a lighter gravy when combined with the pineapple, cloves, and dark brown sugar.

1 (12-pound) bone-in, shank-end ham

½ cup whole cloves

1 (20-ounce) can pineapple rings in their own juice

¾ cup packed dark brown sugar

1 (20-ounce) bottle ginger ale

1 (4-ounce) jar gluten-free maraschino cherries, drained

2 tablespoons cornstarch

¼ cup cold water

1. Preheat oven to 325 degrees F.

2. Place ham in a roasting pan. Using a paring knife, score the rind of the ham into a diamond pattern. Be sure to cut through the skin and fat. Press one clove into the center of each diamond.

3. Drain the juice of the pineapple rings into a bowl and stir in the brown sugar and soda. Pour this mixture over the ham to coat.

4. Arrange the pineapple rings on the outside of the ham, securing each one with a plain wooden toothpick. Place a cherry in the center of each pineapple ring, securing each with a toothpick.

5. Bake uncovered in the oven for four hours, or until internal temperature reaches 160 degrees F. Baste frequently so the cut side of the ham does not get dry.

6. If ham starts to brown too much after three hours, cover the ham with aluminum foil and lower oven temperature to 300 degrees F.

7. Let ham rest, remove to a cutting board and pour off the gravy into a small saucepan. Thicken the gravy with cornstarch dissolved in cold water. Whisk cornstarch into the gravy over a low heat and stir until it thickens.

Nutritional information: 282 calories, 12 grams of protein, 20.6 grams of carbohydrates, 17 grams of fat, 46.7 milligrams of cholesterol, 801 milligrams of sodium, <1 gram of fiber, 20.6 milligrams of calcium, <1 milligram of iron

Allergen Notes and Additional Allergen Substitutions

- To keep gluten free, make sure the ginger ale does not contain barley malt or other gluten-containing ingredients.

TIP: Use cola instead of ginger ale if you are looking for a darker sauce and an even sweeter flavor.

Brisket with Cranberry-Chili Glaze   SERVES 12

GF, MF, EF, SF*, NF, PF, FF, SFF

It may take hours to cook brisket, but once you taste the unbelievably tender meat it will have been worth the wait. Chili adds a unique twist and some heat to the sweet cranberry sauce. This recipe is modified from my friends Marilyn and Darlene's family favorite.

4 pounds uncooked beef brisket with two-thirds of the fat trimmed off

1 large onion, chopped

8 ounces baby carrots

½ cup water

1 teaspoon salt

1 teaspoon pepper

2 teaspoons garlic powder

1 teaspoon onion powder

1 (12-ounce) bottle gluten-free chili sauce

1 (14-ounce) can jellied cranberry sauce

8 ounces whole cranberry sauce

1. Preheat oven to 300 degrees F.

2. Place brisket fat side up in a large oven-safe roasting pan.

3. Cover brisket with onions and carrots. Pour the water into the pan.

4. In a small bowl, combine salt, pepper, garlic powder, onion powder, chili sauce, and cranberry sauce. Pour over brisket.

5. Put brisket pan on top of a baking sheet and cover with aluminum foil.

6. Bake for three to three-and-a-half hours, basting regularly, until brisket is fork-tender.

7. Uncover, bake for an additional 30 minutes, and serve.

Nutritional information: 332 calories, 33.7 grams of protein, 30 grams of carbohydrates, 7.8 grams of fat, 101.5 milligrams of cholesterol, 743 milligrams of sodium, 3.5 grams of fiber, 44 milligrams of calcium, 3.8 milligrams of iron

Allergen Notes and Additional Allergen Substitutions

• To keep soy free, check the chili sauce for soy.

TIP: Make sure you don't buy a brisket that has been seasoned for corned beef.

Stir-Fried Rice Noodles with Peanuts

SERVES 6

GF, MF EF, NF, FF, SFF, V, VG

Since it's difficult to find gluten-free options in Asian restaurants, I created this rice noodle dish that was inspired by pad Thai. With lots of crunchy fresh vegetables and an addictive peanut sauce, you'll never feel left out again.

For the noodles:

8 ounces wide rice noodles (thin rice pasta can be used as well)

1 teaspoon vegetable oil

1½ teaspoons minced garlic

1 teaspoon grated fresh ginger

2 cups shredded cabbage

4 green onions, sliced

1 cup grated carrots

2 cups sugar snap peas

¼ cup gluten-free unsalted vegetable broth

2 tablespoons chopped fresh basil

Chopped peanuts, for garnish

For the sauce:

¼ cup gluten-free unsalted vegetable broth

2 tablespoons sesame oil

2 tablespoons creamy peanut butter

3 tablespoons brown sugar

2 tablespoons gluten-free soy sauce

1. *To make the noodles:* Place noodles in a bowl, cover with boiling water, and let sit for 8 to 10 minutes. Drain and set aside.

2. Heat vegetable oil in a large nonstick skillet or wok over medium-high heat. Add garlic and ginger and sauté for 30 seconds. Add cabbage, green onions, carrots,

snap peas, and ¼ cup vegetable broth. Cook until vegetables are just tender, about three to four minutes.

3. *To make the sauce:* In a small bowl, whisk together ¼ cup vegetable broth, sesame oil, peanut butter, brown sugar, soy sauce, and red pepper flakes.

4. Add sauce and noodles to wok, toss to coat, and heat through. Add basil and garnish with chopped peanuts, if desired. Serve hot or at room temperature.

Nutritional information: 277.2 calories, 5.6 grams of protein, 44.4 grams of carbohydrates, 8.2 grams of fat, 0 milligrams of cholesterol, 323.9 milligrams of sodium, 3.3 grams of fiber, 57.9 milligrams of calcium, 1.1 milligrams of iron

FODMAPs

- To make FODMAP friendly, omit the garlic and substitute bok choy for the cabbage and granulated sugar for the brown sugar.

TIP: Use any variety of vegetables in this dish.

 *Quick and easy*

Lemon Chicken SERVES 4

GF, EF, SF*, NF, PF, FF, SFF

This dish is perfect when cooking for a crowd because the longer the chicken stays in the lemon and white wine sauce the more flavorful and tender it becomes.

1 pound of chicken tenders, cleaned

⅓ cup rice flour

½ teaspoon salt

¼ teaspoon pepper

Gluten-free cooking spray

3 tablespoons butter, divided

2 chopped shallots

¼ cup white wine

2 tablespoons lemon juice

2 tablespoons capers

½ cup reduced-sodium gluten-free chicken broth

1 lemon sliced into ⅛-inch-thick rounds

1. Place one layer of chicken between two sheets of plastic wrap and pound until about ¼-inch thick.

2. In a small bowl, combine flour, salt, and pepper.

3. Dredge chicken tenders through flour mixture, coating each side evenly.

4. Spray a large skillet with cooking spray and place over medium heat until hot. Add 1½ tablespoons of butter.

5. When butter is melted, turn heat to medium-high and add half of the chicken pieces in a single layer (do not crowd). Cook for about four to five minutes on each side, until chicken is lightly browned. Remove and set aside. Melt remaining butter in the skillet and cook remaining chicken. Remove, and set aside with first batch.

6. Add shallots to the skillet and sauté for two minutes. Add wine, lemon juice, capers, lemon slices, chicken broth, and chicken tenders to the pan.

7. Simmer for five minutes, until chicken is cooked through (juices run clear) and the sauce thickens.

Nutritional information: 351.5 calories, 25.8 grams of protein, 16.3 grams of carbohydrates, 19.6 grams of fat, 95.4 milligrams of cholesterol, 568.7 milligrams of sodium, 2 grams of fiber, 40.7 milligrams of calcium, 1.3 milligrams of iron

Allergen Notes and Additional Allergen Substitutions

- To keep soy free, use soy-free cooking spray and check the chicken broth for soy.
- To make milk free, substitute margarine for the butter.

FODMAPs

- To make FODMAP friendly, substitute chopped green onions (green part only) for the shallots.

TIP: This recipe also works well with veal or pork cutlets.

Linguini with Shrimp and Petite Diced Tomatoes SERVES 4

GF, EF*, SF*, NF, PF, FF

I always keep a few cans of petite diced tomatoes in my pantry. They cook quickly while still providing incredible flavor. I use them in many pasta dishes, but this is one of my favorites.

Gluten-free cooking spray

1 tablespoon olive oil

1 small onion, finely chopped

2 tablespoons minced garlic

¼ cup chopped fresh basil

2 teaspoons sugar

¼ cup white wine

1 (28-ounce) can petite diced tomatoes

1 (10-ounce) package frozen broccoli florets, defrosted and drained

1 pound large uncooked shrimp, peeled and deveined

2½ cups cooked gluten-free linguini noodles

2 tablespoons Parmesan cheese

1. Spray a large pot with cooking spray and heat over medium heat. Add olive oil.

2. Sauté onion until translucent. Add garlic, basil, sugar, and white wine and cook for three to four minutes.

3. Add the tomatoes and cook for 15 minutes. Add broccoli and shrimp and cook for four to five minutes, or until all shrimp have turned pink. Add linguini noodles and toss.

4. Remove from heat, sprinkle with Parmesan cheese, and serve. Garnish with additional fresh basil if desired.

Nutritional information: 310 calories, 22.9 grams of protein, 48.7 grams of carbohydrates, 6.6 grams of fat, 137 milligrams of cholesterol, 563 milligrams of sodium, 7 grams of fiber, 185.8 milligrams of calcium, 2.7 milligrams of iron

Allergen Notes and Additional Allergen Substitutions

- To keep soy free, use soy-free cooking spray and check the pasta for soy.

- To keep egg free, check the pasta for eggs.

- To make milk free, omit Parmesan cheese.

FODMAPs

- To make FODMAP friendly, substitute spinach for the broccoli and garlic-infused oil (page 31) for the minced garlic.

TIP: As an alternative to the shrimp, substitute 2-inch pieces of chicken breast—add in step 3, and extend cooking time until chicken is cooked through (juices run clear).

Hawaiian Chicken   SERVES 8

GF, MF, EF, NF, PF, FF, SFF

Hawaii is one of the most beautiful places I have ever visited: beautiful beaches, awe-inspiring volcanoes, and amazing luaus. This dish brings me back there every time.

2 pounds chicken cutlets or chicken tenders

½ cup rice flour

1 teaspoon salt

⅛ teaspoon pepper

¼ cup olive or corn oil

1 large green pepper, cut crosswise into ¼ inch circles

1 cup baby carrots, boiled until tender

1 (16-ounce) jar pineapple in syrup, sliced or in chunks, syrup reserved

For the sauce:

Reserved pineapple syrup

1 cup granulated sugar

2 tablespoons cornstarch

¾ cup cider vinegar

1 tablespoon gluten-free soy sauce

¼ teaspoon ginger

1 gluten-free chicken bouillon cube or packet

1. Preheat oven to 350 degrees F.

2. Prepare cutlets by trimming and cutting into pieces or strips. Season rice flour with salt and pepper. Coat chicken with rice flour mixture.

3. Heat oil in a large skillet over medium-high heat. Add chicken and brown on all sides. Remove to a shallow roasting pan.

4. *To make the sauce:* Pour reserved pineapple syrup into a 2-cup measuring cup. Add enough water to make 1¼ cups total.

5. In a medium saucepan, combine pineapple syrup, sugar, cornstarch, vinegar, gluten-free soy sauce, ginger, and bouillon. Bring to a boil, stirring constantly, for two minutes. Pour over chicken. Add peppers and carrots.

6. Bake, uncovered, for 20 minutes. Add pineapple and cook 20 minutes longer.

Nutritional information: 406.3 calories, 26.8 grams of protein, 51.4 grams of carbohydrates, 9.9 grams of fat, 82.7 milligrams of cholesterol, 607.4 milligrams of sodium, 1.5 grams of fiber, 24 milligrams of calcium, 1 milligram of iron

Allergen Notes and Additional Allergen Substitutions

- To make soy free, omit soy sauce, add 1 teaspoon salt, and check the chicken bouillon for soy.

TIP: Serve with rice, millet, or quinoa.

Chicken with Mushrooms and Cream Sauce   SERVES 4

GF, EF, SF*, NF, PF, FF, SFF

A dreamy dish of tender chicken in a light cream sauce studded with mushrooms.

- 2 tablespoons salted butter
- 2 tablespoons minced garlic
- 1 pound of uncooked chicken tenders (cleaned, with any white muscle removed) or chicken cutlets
- ¼ cup rice flour
- ½ teaspoon sea salt
- ¼ cup white wine
- ½ cup gluten-free chicken broth
- 4 ounces sliced fresh mushrooms
- ¼ teaspoon dried thyme
- 4 tablespoons gluten-free, fat-free half-and-half
- 2 tablespoons Parmesan cheese
- 2 tablespoons chopped fresh parsley

1. Melt butter in a large skillet over medium heat. Sauté garlic for two to three minutes, until it starts to brown.

2. Meanwhile, combine rice flour and salt in a small bowl. Toss chicken in mixture and coat well. Brown chicken in skillet until just cooked. Remove from pan and set aside.

3. Deglaze pan with white wine and chicken broth.

4. Add mushrooms and thyme and simmer until mushrooms are cooked. Add cooked chicken, half-and-half, and Parmesan cheese to the skillet. Simmer until sauce thickens.

5. To serve, spoon sauce over chicken and garnish with chopped parsley.

Nutritional information: 277.1 calories, 29.1 grams of protein, 11.6 grams of carbohydrates, 11.6 grams of fat, 108.9 milligrams of cholesterol, 468.2 milligrams of sodium, <1 gram of fiber, 59 milligrams of calcium, <1 milligram of iron

Allergen Notes and Additional Allergen Substitutions

- To keep soy free, check chicken broth for soy.
- To make milk free, substitute margarine for the butter, substitute rice milk for the half-and-half, and use a dairy-free cheese.

TIPS: You can adjust the amount of garlic and mushrooms as desired. Chopped sun-dried tomatoes and sweet peas are excellent additions.

Macaroni and Cheese SERVES 6

GF*, EF*, SF, NF, PF, FF, SFF, V

Pureed cauliflower adds flavor, a nutritional boost, and even more creaminess to this dish. Serve as a side dish or as a main course with salad as a side.

1 tablespoon olive oil

1 clove garlic, minced

2 cups cauliflower florets

1 cup water

1 cup half-and-half

½ teaspoon sea salt

¼ teaspoon black pepper

½ teaspoon gluten-free dry mustard powder

½ cup shredded, extra sharp cheddar cheese

½ cup shredded, part-skim mozzarella cheese

2 tablespoons chopped fresh chives

1 tablespoon chopped fresh parsley

4 cups cooked gluten-free pasta (I recommend elbow-shaped rice pasta)

1. Preheat oven to 350 degrees F.

2. Heat oil in a large saucepan over medium heat. Add garlic and cauliflower. Cook, stirring frequently, until garlic is just starting to brown.

3. Add water, reduce heat, and simmer until cauliflower is tender.

4. Puree cauliflower in a blender, or batched in a food processor, until smooth. (Remember to use caution when pureeing hot liquids.) Return to saucepan and add half-and-half, salt, pepper, and mustard.

5. Stir in cheeses until melted. Add chives and parsley and fold in cooked pasta. Pour into a 2-quart casserole dish and bake for 30 minutes, until hot and bubbly.

Nutritional information: 291 calories, 15.2 grams of protein, 32.6 grams of carbohydrates, 11.7 grams of fat, 33.6 milligrams of cholesterol, 460 milligrams of sodium, 2 grams of fiber, 334.7 milligrams of calcium, 1 milligram of iron

Allergen Notes and Additional Allergen Substitutions

- To keep gluten free, check packaged shredded cheeses for gluten-containing anti-caking agents.
- To keep egg free, check the pasta for eggs.

TIP: To vary the flavor, try different cheeses such as Muenster, Monterrey Jack, or Romano.

Braised Short Ribs SERVES 10

GF, MF, EF, SF*, NF, PF, FF, SFF

Every time I make this dish someone asks me for the recipe. Serve with garlic mashed potatoes (page 64).

2 tablespoons olive oil

6 pounds short ribs, meaty and thick

1 cup of chopped carrots

2 celery stalks, chopped

2 onions, chopped

8 medium shallots, chopped

4 ounces tomato paste

¼ cup rice flour

Bouquet garni (1 head garlic cut in half crosswise, 2 sprigs parsley, 1 sprig thyme, 1 to 2 bay leafs, 3 to 4 peppercorns, and 2 cloves, tied in cheesecloth)

1 bottle (750 ml) full-bodied red wine such as a cabernet or merlot

1½ cups red port wine

⅓ cup granulated sugar

1 cup raisins or currants

4 cups low-sodium, gluten-free veal or beef broth

1 teaspoon salt

½ teaspoon pepper

1 teaspoon garlic powder

1 teaspoon onion powder

1. In a large pot or Dutch oven, heat oil over medium-high heat. Add meat and brown on all sides. Remove and set aside.

2. In the same pan, sauté carrots, celery, onions, and shallots for 5 to 10 minutes, until browned. Add tomato paste and rice flour, cooking three to four minutes, scraping the bottom of the pan to stir in any brown bits.

3. Add browned meat, bouquet garni, wine, port, sugar, and raisins to the pan. Increase heat and cook until volume is reduced by half.

4. Add stock and bring to a boil. Lower heat a little, cover, and cook for about three hours or until meat is fork-tender.

5. Reduce temperature to low. Add salt, pepper, garlic powder, and onion powder and cook for 10 minutes.

6. Remove meat to a platter and cover.

7. Strain the sauce, boil it down until it thickens, then taste and season as desired. Pour over meat and serve.

Nutritional information: 556.3 calories, 37.8 grams of protein, 30 grams of carbohydrates, 21.4 grams of fat, 107 milligrams of cholesterol, 511.5 milligrams of sodium, 2.4 grams of fiber, 54 milligrams of calcium, 5.7 milligrams of iron

Allergen Notes and Additional Allergen Substitutions

*   To keep soy free, check broth for soy.

TIP: I usually prep and store veggies and ingredients in the refrigerator ahead of time so everything is ready and assembling this dish is a breeze.

 *Quick and easy*

Turkey Meat Loaf SERVES 8

GF, MF*, SF*, NF, PF, FF, SFF

Step aside chewy, flavorless turkey meat loaf. Moist and well-seasoned, this version finishes under the broiler to caramelize the top.

- 1½ pounds of ground breast of turkey
- 1 medium onion, chopped
- 1 celery stalk, chopped
- 1 tablespoon minced garlic
- ½ teaspoon garlic powder
- ½ teaspoon onion powder
- 1 teaspoon salt
- ½ teaspoon pepper
- 4 tablespoons gluten-free ketchup
- ¾ cup coarse, gluten-free bread crumbs
- 1 egg slightly beaten
- 2 egg whites

1. In a microwave, cook chopped onion for one-and-a-half minutes on high to soften slightly.
2. Preheat oven to 375 degrees F.
3. Thoroughly mix all the ingredients together.
4. Place meat loaf into a large loaf pan.
5. Cook until internal temperature reaches 170 degrees F, about one hour.
6. When cooked through, turn oven to broil and broil for about five minutes, until surface is golden brown and excess liquid is absorbed.

Nutritional information: 153.5 calories, 23.2 grams of protein, 11.6 grams of carbohydrates, 1.4 grams of fat, 64.5 milligrams of cholesterol, 484.7 milligrams of sodium, <1 gram of fiber, 13.9 milligrams of calcium, <1 milligram of iron

Allergen Notes and Additional Allergen Substitutions

- To keep soy free and milk free, check bread crumbs for soy and milk.
- To make egg free, check bread crumbs for egg and use a gluten-free, eggless egg substitute.

FODMAPs

- To make FODMAP friendly, replace garlic powder, onion powder, and minced garlic with 1 tablespoon of garlic-infused oil (page 31) and two chopped green onions (green part only). Omit celery and substitute tomato sauce mixed with 1 tablespoon of granulated sugar for the ketchup.

TIP: Uncooked meat loaf mixture can be made into turkey burgers and meatballs.

Oven-Baked "Fried" Chicken   SERVES 6

GF, EF, SF, NF, PF, FF, SFF

Baking in a roasting pan crisps the chicken without the mess of frying!

3 pounds cut-up whole chicken, skin removed

1 cup buttermilk (or 1 cup whole milk mixed with 1 tablespoon white vinegar)

1 teaspoon cayenne pepper

2 tablespoons olive oil

2 tablespoons unsalted butter

⅔ cup white rice flour

⅓ cup tapioca flour

½ teaspoon black pepper

2 teaspoons paprika

½ teaspoon salt

1. Place chicken in a large, sealable plastic bag with buttermilk and cayenne pepper. Place in refrigerator to marinate for one to two hours.

2. Preheat oven to 400 degrees F.

3. Place olive oil and butter in a 9 × 13-inch pan and place in oven until butter has melted. Swirl mixture around pan to make sure the bottom is evenly coated.

4. Place rice flour, tapioca flour, pepper, paprika, and salt in a shallow dish.

5. Shake excess buttermilk off each piece of chicken and dip in flour mixture until completely coated. Place in prepared pan.

6. Bake in the oven for 30 minutes. Turn each piece over and bake for an additional 20 minutes, or until cooked through (juices run clear).

Nutritional information: 282 calories, 26 grams of protein, 15.6 grams of carbohydrates, 12.3 grams of fat, 90 milligrams of cholesterol, 127 milligrams of sodium, <1 gram of fiber, 42.6 milligrams of calcium, 1.3 milligrams of iron

Allergen Notes and Additional Allergen Substitutions

- To make milk free, substitute margarine for the butter and rice, coconut, or almond milk mixed with 1 tablespoon white vinegar for the buttermilk.

FODMAPs

- To make FODMAP friendly, substitute lactose-free, rice, or coconut milk mixed with 1 tablespoon white vinegar for the buttermilk.

TIP: If you are watching your salt intake, substitute your favorite Mrs. Dash salt-free seasoning for the salt.

One-Dish Dinners

W ho has unlimited time anymore? Not me. One dish meals save time and money, and leftovers keep well in the refrigerator or freezer. These are the dishes to bring to your next potluck.

Broccoli and Cheese Casserole

Chickpeas with Butternut Squash and Spinach

Eggplant and Rice Casserole

Shrimp Risotto

Homemade Manicotti

Slow-Cooked White Chicken Chili

Homemade Cheese Ravioli

Shepherd's Pie

Pasta e Fagioli

Turkey a la King

Deep-Dish Chicken Pot Pie

Broccoli and Cheese Casserole SERVES 6

GF, EF, SF*, NF, PF, FF, SFF, V

Vegetable casseroles are too often overlooked as a main. This hearty dish stands on its own, but if you want a more substantial entrée, add a layer of quinoa or beans to the casserole.

4 cups fresh broccoli florets

Gluten-free cooking spray or 1 teaspoon olive oil

2 tablespoons plus 2 teaspoons olive oil, divided

2 tablespoons unsalted butter

½ cup chopped onion

1 tablespoon minced garlic

3 tablespoons tapioca flour

1 cup gluten-free vegetable broth

1 cup 2% milk

1 teaspoon sea salt, divided

½ teaspoon pepper, divided

½ teaspoon paprika

½ cup shredded Monterey Jack cheese

½ cup shredded, reduced-fat cheddar cheese

1 cup gluten-free cornflakes

1. Place 1 inch of water and broccoli in a medium saucepan. Bring to a boil, then reduce heat and simmer for three to five minutes, until crisp-tender. Drain and set aside.

2. Preheat oven to 350 degrees F. Spray a 2-quart casserole dish with nonstick cooking spray.

3. Heat 2 tablespoons olive oil and butter in a large, heavy saucepan. Add onions and garlic and sauté for five minutes, until garlic is lightly browned. Whisk in tapioca flour until well-combined.

4. Whisk in vegetable broth, milk, ½ teaspoon salt, ¼ teaspoon pepper, and paprika. Reduce heat and simmer until sauce is thickened. Remove from heat and stir in cheese until melted.

5. In a food processor, combine cornflakes, remaining olive oil, salt, and pepper. Blend until crushed.

6. Place broccoli in casserole dish, add the sauce, and top with crumbs. Bake, uncovered, for 30 minutes.

Nutritional information: 223 calories, 8.4 grams of protein, 15.9 grams of carbohydrates, 14.5 grams of fat, 24 milligrams of cholesterol, 592 milligrams of sodium, 1 gram of fiber, 195 milligrams of calcium, <1 milligram of iron

Allergen Notes and Additional Allergen Substitutions

- To keep soy free, use olive oil or soy-free cooking spray and check the vegetable broth and cornflakes for soy.

TIP: This recipe can be made ahead It will keep for several days when refrigerated and covered. Heat in the oven or microwave, covered, until bubbling.

Chickpeas with Butternut Squash and Spinach   SERVES 4

GF, MF, EF, SF, NF, PF, FF, SFF, V, VG

Garlic, ginger, and chili add zip to this healthful vegetarian dish, and the chickpeas provide a nice texture.

2 teaspoons olive oil

1 cup chopped onion

1 tablespoon minced garlic

1 tablespoon grated fresh ginger

1 cup water

3 tablespoons tomato paste

2 cups thinly sliced and peeled butternut squash

2 cups chopped fresh spinach

2 teaspoons chili powder

¼ teaspoon salt

1 (15.5 ounce) can chickpeas, rinsed and drained

1 tablespoon fresh lemon juice

Grated lemon zest

1. Heat oil in a large nonstick skillet over medium-high heat. Add onion, garlic, and ginger. Cook, stirring frequently, until mixture begins to brown.

2. Add water and tomato paste. Stir to combine. Add squash. Reduce heat and simmer for six to eight minutes, until the squash is almost cooked through and most of the liquid has evaporated.

3. Stir in spinach, chili powder, salt, and chickpeas. Cover and cook for five minutes longer, until spinach wilts and mixture is heated through.

4. Remove from heat. Stir in lemon juice, sprinkle with zest, and serve.

Nutritional information: 168 calories, 6.7 grams of protein, 28.5 grams of carbohydrates, 4.4 grams of fat, 0 milligrams of cholesterol, 460 milligrams of sodium, 7.4 grams of fiber, 99.6 milligrams of calcium, 2.7 milligrams of iron

FODMAPs

- To make FODMAP friendly, substitute six chopped green onions (green part only) for the onions, 1 tablespoon of garlic-infused oil (page 31) for the fresh or minced garlic, and ¼ cup of tomato sauce for the tomato paste.

TIP: This dish can also be served cold.

Eggplant and Rice Casserole   SERVES 12

GF, EF, SF*, NF, PF, FF, SFF

A layer of rice adds complexity to this variation of eggplant Parmesan.

For the sauce:

> ½ cup olive oil, divided
>
> 2 medium onions, chopped
>
> 2 tablespoons chopped garlic
>
> 1 (6-ounce) can tomato paste
>
> 2½ cups water
>
> ½ teaspoon basil
>
> 1 teaspoon salt
>
> ½ teaspoon pepper
>
> 1¼ cups gluten-free beef broth
>
> 4 tablespoons salted butter, softened

For the casserole:

> 1 large eggplant, peeled and cut into ¼-inch slices
>
> 1 cup uncooked rice
>
> ¼ pound part-skim mozzarella cheese, grated
>
> ¼ cup grated Parmesan cheese

1. *To make the sauce:* Heat ¼ cup of olive oil in a large skillet over medium heat. Add onions and garlic and sauté until the onions are translucent.

2. Add the tomato paste, water, basil, salt, and pepper. Simmer, uncovered, for 30 minutes.

3. Add beef broth, cover, and simmer for 20 minutes.

4. Add the butter and adjust seasonings to taste. Remove sauce from heat and set aside.

5. Preheat oven to 350 degrees F.

6. Heat remaining olive oil in a large skillet over medium-high heat. Cook the eggplant slices until browned on both sides. Drain on paper towels.

7. Pour one-third of the sauce into a large casserole dish. Layer half of the rice over the sauce, add a layer of eggplant in overlapping slices, and follow with a layer of half of the mozzarella. Repeat with second layers of sauce, rice, eggplant, and cheese, and finish with a layer of sauce.

8. Sprinkle with Parmesan cheese.

9. Bake for 45 to 55 minutes, until browned and crusty on top. Sauce will be bubbling and rice will be cooked.

Nutritional information: 229 calories, 6 grams of protein, 23 grams of carbohydrates, 13.2 grams of fat, 12.6 milligrams of cholesterol, 344 milligrams of sodium, 2.9 grams of fiber, 118 milligrams of calcium, 1.4 milligrams of iron

Allergen Notes and Additional Allergen Substitutions

- To keep soy free, check the beef broth for soy.
- To make vegetarian, substitute vegetable broth for the beef broth.

TIP: Zucchini is an excellent alternative to the eggplant in this recipe.

Shrimp Risotto   SERVES 6

GF, EF, SF*, NF, PF, FF

A classic Italian rice dish. Take care not to overcook the shrimp. Magnifico!

2 tablespoons olive oil

1 pound large shrimp, peeled and deveined

¼ teaspoon sea salt

½ teaspoon black pepper

½ cup chopped onion

1 teaspoon minced garlic

1 cup uncooked Arborio rice

½ cup dry white wine (optional)

3 cups gluten-free, low sodium chicken broth

1 cup sweet green peas

¼ cup grated Parmesan cheese

2 tablespoons chopped fresh parsley

1 tablespoon chopped fresh basil

1 teaspoon grated lemon zest

1. Heat 1 tablespoon of olive oil in a large saucepan over medium heat. Add the shrimp and sprinkle with salt and pepper. Cook until the shrimp are just opaque in the center, about three minutes. Transfer the shrimp to a bowl to cool.

2. Return the pan to the heat. Add remaining olive oil. Add onion and garlic and sauté for about three minutes, until onions are softened and garlic is lightly browned.

3. Add the rice and stir until coated, one minute. Add the wine, if using, and cook until the wine is absorbed.

4. Add ½ cup of the broth to the rice, stirring constantly until liquid is absorbed. When the rice is almost dry, add another ½ cup of broth and repeat the process. Continue adding broth until the rice is tender and all the liquid is absorbed—about 35 minutes.

5. Stir in the peas, Parmesan cheese, parsley, basil, lemon zest, and cooked shrimp. Serve immediately.

Nutritional information: 238 calories, 15.3 grams of protein, 29.1 grams of carbohydrates, 6.6 grams of fat, 69.6 milligrams of cholesterol, 656.9 milligrams of sodium, 1.8 grams of fiber, 77 milligrams of calcium, <1 milligram of iron

Allergen Notes and Additional Allergen Substitutions

- To keep soy free, check the chicken broth for soy.
- To make milk free, use a dairy-free cheese.

FODMAPs

- To make FODMAP friendly, substitute chopped green onions (green part only) for the onion and garlic-infused oil (page 31) for the garlic.

TIP: Risotto turns glutinous when held too long, so you should serve it right away.

Homemade Manicotti SERVES 9

GF, SF*, NF, PF, FF, SFF, V

Fresh pasta is easy to make, and these delicate manicotti will melt in your mouth. Using lower-fat cheese makes a real difference in holding down the fat content.

For manicotti shells:

1 cup white rice flour

½ cup tapioca flour

¼ teaspoon sea salt

4 eggs

1½ cups water

Gluten-free cooking spray or 1 teaspoon olive oil

For the filling:

2 cups part-skim ricotta cheese

1½ cups shredded, part-skim mozzarella cheese, divided

2 tablespoons grated Parmesan cheese

1 tablespoon chopped fresh parsley

1 tablespoon chopped fresh basil

2 cups marinara sauce (page 117)

1. *To make shells:* Blend flours, salt, eggs, and water in a blender or food processor until smooth.

2. Spray an 8-inch skillet with cooking spray and heat over medium heat.

3. Pour 2 tablespoons batter into center of skillet. Tilt the pan with a circular motion so the batter coats the surface evenly. Cook until just set, about one minute. Do not turn or brown. Remove from pan.

4. Repeat with remaining batter, spraying pan when necessary to prevent sticking, making 18 crepes. Stack crepes with waxed paper and set aside.

5. *To make filling:* Mix ricotta cheese, 1 cup mozzarella cheese, Parmesan cheese, parsley, and basil in a large bowl.

6. To assemble, place 3 to 4 tablespoons of the cheese mixture in the center of each shell. Roll up. Place 1 cup marinara sauce in the bottom of a 13 x 9-inch baking dish. Place manicotti seam side down in dish. Cover with remaining sauce and sprinkle with remaining mozzarella cheese.

7. Cover with aluminum foil and bake for 20 minutes. Uncover and bake for an additional 15 minutes to allow the cheese to brown. Serve warm with extra grated Parmesan cheese on top, if desired.

Nutritional information: 338 calories, 18.6 grams of protein, 32.1 grams of carbohydrates, 14.1 grams of fat, 128 milligrams of cholesterol, 584 milligrams of sodium, 1.9 grams of fiber, 383 milligrams of calcium, 1.5 milligrams of iron

Allergen Notes and Additional Allergen Substitutions
- To keep soy free, use olive oil or soy-free cooking spray.
- To make egg free, use a gluten-free, eggless egg substitute.

TIP: This is a great make-ahead dish. Wrap the crepes in plastic and store for up to two days in the refrigerator. Or you can prepare the recipe through step 6, cover, and refrigerate to bake within two days (if kept any longer, the pasta may get soggy).

Slow-Cooked White Chicken Chili   SERVES 6

GF, EF, SF, NF, PF, FF, SFF

Give this a try on football Sunday. A change from traditional, heavy, tomato-based chili, this version features chunks of white chicken and cannellini beans in a spicy broth seasoned with cilantro and cumin.

1 tablespoon olive oil

1 cup chopped onion

1 tablespoon minced garlic

2 whole boneless, skinless chicken breasts (about 1 pound)

¼ teaspoon sea salt

½ teaspoon black pepper

1 (4.5-ounce) can diced green chili peppers

1 (30-ounce) can white cannellini beans, rinsed and drained

2 teaspoons ground cumin

½ teaspoon dried oregano

2 cups gluten-free unsalted chicken broth

¼ cup shredded Monterey Jack cheese

2 tablespoons chopped fresh cilantro

Lime wedges (optional)

1. Heat oil in a medium skillet over medium-high heat. Add onion and sauté for two minutes. Add garlic and sauté for one to two minutes longer. Place in a slow cooker.

2. Sprinkle chicken with salt and pepper. Add to skillet and brown on both sides.

3. Add chili peppers, beans, cumin, and oregano to slow cooker. Place chicken on top of beans in slow cooker. Pour broth over chicken and cook on low for six hours. Turn off the slow cooker.

4. Remove 1 cup of beans and ½ cup liquid from slow cooker and puree in a blender or food processor. Return to slow cooker and mix until well combined. Remove chicken, shred it, return it to slow cooker, and mix to combine.

5. Spoon into individual serving bowls. Sprinkle with cheese and cilantro, add lime wedge, and serve.

Nutritional information: 277.7 calories, 27.2 grams of protein, 23.7 grams of carbohydrates, 7.2 grams of fat, 57.1 milligrams of cholesterol, 401.8 milligrams of sodium, 7.3 grams of fiber, 150.8 milligrams of calcium, 2.9 milligrams of iron

Allergen Notes and Additional Allergen Substitutions

- To make milk free, omit the cheese or use a dairy-free cheese.

TIPS: This recipe doubles easily. It can also be prepared ahead of time and reheated on the stove. Store in the refrigerator for up to three days or in the freezer for up to four months.

Homemade Cheese Ravioli SERVES 6

GF, SF, NF, PF, FF, SFF, V

I find homemade gluten-free pasta easier to make than its gluten-containing counterpart. It doesn't fight you when you are rolling it out, and you can rework it as much as you like without it getting tough. Top these airy ravioli with your favorite sauce, and enjoy.

For the pasta:

⅓ cup sweet rice flour

⅔ cup sorghum flour

½ cup white rice flour

½ cup cornstarch

2 teaspoons xanthan gum

1 teaspoon sea salt

2 eggs

3 egg yolks

2 tablespoons olive oil

3 to 4 tablespoons ice water

For the filling:

1 cup part-skim ricotta cheese

1 egg

¼ cup shredded part-skim mozzarella cheese

1 tablespoon chopped fresh parsley

1 tablespoon chopped fresh basil

1. *To make pasta:* Whisk together flours, cornstarch, xanthan gum, and sea salt.

2. Make a well in the center of the flour mixture. Add eggs, egg yolks, and olive oil. Mix ingredients, using a fork or your hands, until the dough comes together. While working the dough, add a little ice water at a time until it feels pliable but firm, like play-doh.

3. Divide the dough into four pieces and roll out until ½-inch thick. Run the dough through a pasta machine, increasing the setting each time, until the dough is paper-thin and long. If rolling by hand, roll out each piece of dough as thin as you can.

4. Cut the rolled out dough into 2-inch squares.

5. *To make the filling:* Mix all ingredients in a small bowl until well blended.

6. To assemble, dollop a heaping teaspoon of the filling onto the middle of a square of pasta. Brush edges with water and place another square of pasta on top. Press down and crimp the edges with a fork or ravioli cutter.

7. To cook, bring a large pot of salted water to a boil. Place ravioli in pot, a few at a time, and cook for four to five minutes, until they rise to the top and you are able to bite into them without having them fall apart.

8. Top with your favorite pasta sauce and serve immediately.

Nutritional information: 340 calories, 12.9 grams of protein, 39.8 grams of carbohydrates, 14 grams of fat, 200 milligrams of cholesterol, 126 milligrams of sodium, 179 milligrams of calcium, 1.8 milligrams of iron, 2.3 grams of fiber

TIPS: Watch carefully when cooking. Cooking times may vary depending on how thin you were able to roll out the dough. If you overcook, ravioli will fall apart and become mushy. You can keep uncooked ravioli covered in the refrigerator for up to a day. Freeze uncooked ravioli on a baking sheet that has been coated with waxed paper (so they don't stick), and place in a freezer bag until ready to use.

Shepherd's Pie   SERVES 6

GF, EF, SF*, NF, PF, FF, SFF

A succulent casserole of beef and vegetables topped with mashed potatoes and a flaky, golden crust.

3 pounds red potatoes

¼ cup low-fat sour cream

1 tablespoon unsalted butter

¾ teaspoon sea salt, divided

½ teaspoon black pepper, divided

1 pound lean ground beef

1½ teaspoons minced garlic

1 cup chopped celery

4 green onions, sliced

1 tablespoon tapioca flour

1 cup gluten-free, low-sodium beef broth

1 tablespoon tomato paste

1 (10-ounce) bag frozen mixed vegetables, defrosted and drained

¼ cup shredded reduced-fat cheddar cheese

1. Preheat oven to 375 degrees F.

2. Peel and dice potatoes. Cook in boiling water until tender, about 15 minutes. Drain and return to pot. Add sour cream, butter, ¼ teaspoon salt, and ¼ teaspoon pepper. Mash until potatoes are smooth and mixture is well blended. Set aside.

3. Brown beef in a large nonstick skillet over medium-high heat. Add garlic, celery, and onions. Cook for three to four minutes, until vegetables start to soften. Add flour, salt, and pepper. Stir together for one minute. Add broth, tomato paste, and vegetables and cook for an additional five minutes, stirring frequently.

4. Spoon meat mixture into six 8-ounce ramekins or casserole dishes. Top with potatoes and bake for 15 minutes. Sprinkle with cheese and bake an additional two to three minutes. Serve immediately.

Nutritional information: 372.7 calories, 23.3 grams of protein, 45.5 grams of carbohydrates, 11.1 grams of fat, 58.1 milligrams of cholesterol, 485.9 milligrams of sodium, 6.4 grams of fiber, 91.4 milligrams of calcium, 4 milligrams of iron

Allergen Notes and Additional Allergen Substitutions

- To keep soy free, check the beef broth for soy.

FODMAPs

- To make FODMAP friendly, omit the garlic, celery, and tomato paste. Replace the frozen vegetables with FODMAP-friendly vegetables such as corn, carrots, and peas.

TIPS: This dish can be prepared in a 2-quart casserole dish instead of individual ramekins. For a lighter shepherd's pie, use ground turkey or chicken instead of beef to reduce the fat. This dish can be prepared and then frozen until you are ready to bake and eat it.

Pasta e Fagioli   SERVES 6
GF, EF*, SF*, NF, PF, FF, SFF

Warming and comforting, this simple, rustic dish is the perfect one-pot meal.

2 tablespoons olive oil

⅛ pound salt pork, chopped fine

1 medium onion, chopped fine

1 celery stalk, chopped fine

2 cloves garlic, minced

1 cup tomato sauce

½ teaspoon sea salt

⅛ teaspoon black pepper

4 cups warm water or gluten-free chicken broth

2 cups cooked white beans (10.5-ounce can with liquid) or 1 cup of dried black-eyed peas, cooked

1½ cups uncooked gluten-free pasta (small elbows or spirals work best)

1 tablespoon fresh parsley, chopped

¼ cup pesto sauce (page 171), or to taste

¼ cup Parmesan cheese

1. Heat oil in a large saucepan. Add pork and sauté until it is no longer pink, two to three minutes.

2. Add onion, celery, and garlic and sauté until onions are golden.

3. Stir in tomato sauce, salt, and pepper and cook for 10 minutes.

4. Add warm water or broth and beans and bring to a boil. Cook for 10 minutes. Add pasta and boil, uncovered, for 15 minutes, or until pasta is tender (stir frequently). Add chopped parsley and pesto until combined. Serve with grated cheese.

🥄 **Nutritional information:** 331 calories, 10.3 grams of protein, 35.2 grams of carbohydrates, 17.2 grams of fat, 11.4 milligrams of cholesterol, 808 milligrams of sodium, 5.8 grams of fiber, 125.3 milligrams of calcium, 3.2 milligrams of iron

Allergen Notes and Additional Allergen Substitutions

- To keep egg free, check the pasta for eggs.
- To keep soy free, check the pasta and chicken broth (if using) for soy.

TIPS: The pasta and beans may soak up a lot of the broth. The soup should be thick but still have enough liquid to eat with a spoon, not a fork. If the soup is too thick, add a little extra water or broth to thin. This soup keeps well in the refrigerator for five days. To reheat, stir in enough boiling water to achieve the desired consistency and heat over low flame. Store this soup in the freezer for up to four months.

 *Quick and easy*

Turkey a la King   SERVES 6

GF, EF, SF*, NF, PF, FF, SFF

When I was a little girl, I loved it when my mom used leftover turkey or chicken to make chicken or turkey a la king. This heavenly dish always hits the spot.

6 cups (48 ounces) of gluten-free, reduced-fat cream soup (such as cream of mushroom, broccoli, or potato)

2 tablespoons tapioca flour or cornstarch

4 cups cooked turkey, cut into 2-inch pieces

1 teaspoon garlic powder

1 teaspoon onion powder

¼ teaspoon sea salt

¼ teaspoon black pepper

4 tablespoons Parmesan cheese

1. In a medium-size pot, heat soup over medium heat. Remove ¼ cup of soup from pot and mix with the tapioca flour or cornstarch. Add back to soup pot and keep stirring over low heat until thickened.

2. Add turkey, garlic powder, and onion powder and heat for five minutes.

3. Add salt, pepper, and Parmesan cheese. Adjust seasonings as desired.

Nutritional information: 256 calories, 31.4 grams of protein, 12.9 grams of carbohydrates, 7.6 grams of fat, 91.7 milligrams of cholesterol, 778 milligrams of sodium, 1 gram of fiber, 47.8 milligrams of calcium, <1 milligram of iron

Allergen Notes and Additional Allergen Substitutions

- To keep soy free, check the soup for soy.

TIPS: To make a lower-fat comfort food, use the white meat only. Serve over cooked rice or quinoa. This dish also works well with added veggies such as sweet peas, broccoli florets, or asparagus tips.

Deep-Dish Chicken Pot Pie SERVES 12

GF, EF, SF*, NF, PF, FF, SFF

I like to bake this luxurious chicken stew topped with a flaky crust in small ramekins so each person gets their own pot pie.

For the crust:

1 cup white rice flour

½ cup tapioca flour

½ teaspoon sea salt

½ cup unsalted butter, cut into small pieces

4 to 6 tablespoons ice water

For the filling:

4 tablespoons olive oil

½ cup finely diced onion

½ cup finely diced celery

1½ teaspoons minced garlic

¼ cup cornstarch

½ teaspoon sea salt

½ teaspoon black pepper

½ cup dry white wine (optional)

3 cups gluten-free, low-sodium chicken broth

3 cups shredded cooked chicken

1 (12-ounce) package frozen mixed vegetables

1 tablespoon chopped fresh thyme

2 tablespoons chopped fresh parsley

¼ cup whole milk

1. *To make the crust:* Combine the flours and salt in a large bowl.

2. Using a pastry blender, cut butter into flour mixture until it resembles coarse crumbs.

3. Add water, 1 tablespoon at a time, continuing to blend until all ingredients are moist.

4. Form dough into a ball and place on one sheet of waxed paper. Place a second sheet of waxed paper on top. Flatten dough with palm of hand, then roll out to an 11- to 12-inch circle, about ⅛-inch thick.

5. *To prepare the filling:* Preheat oven to 375 degrees F.

6. Heat oil in a large pot over medium heat. Add onion, celery, and garlic. Cook and stir for about three minutes, until onions start to turn translucent.

7. Stir in cornstarch, salt, and pepper for one minute. Add chicken broth and wine if using. Continue to cook and stir until mixture starts to thicken.

8. Stir in chicken, mixed vegetables, thyme, parsley, and milk. Cook for an additional three minutes, until bubbly and thick. Remove from heat.

9. To assemble, pour chicken mixture into a 10-inch deep-dish pie plate. Remove top sheet of waxed paper from crust and lay dough over top of dish. Remove second sheet of waxed paper. Press the dough so that the edges stick to pie plate. Use a knife to cut three to four small vents in the surface of the dough.

10. Bake for 25 to 30 minutes, until crust is browned and filling is bubbling.

Nutritional information: 273 calories, 14 grams of protein, 22.1 grams of carbohydrates, 14.1 grams of fat, 50.6 milligrams of cholesterol, 255.2 milligrams of sodium, 1.8 grams of fiber, 30 milligrams of calcium, <1 milligram of iron

Allergen Notes and Additional Allergen Substitutions

- To keep soy free, check the chicken broth for soy.
- To make milk free, substitute rice milk for the milk and margarine for the butter.

TIP: Use turkey in place of chicken and vary the vegetables.

Recipe Directory with Allergy and FODMAP Information

Use this directory as a quick reference to find pertinent allergy information and potential modifications for all of the recipes in this book.

The codes are: QE = quick and easy, GF = gluten free, MF = milk free, SF = soy free, EF = egg free, NF = nut free, PF = peanut free, FF = fish free, SFF = shellfish free, V = vegetarian, VG = vegan, LFM = low FODMAP.

X = allergen omitted from recipe or low in FODMAPs
P = it is possible to adapt the recipe to omit this allergen or make it low in FODMAPs

> **I have utilized current resources to provide allergy recommendations. Since ingredients often change, always read labels and call manufacturers on any questionable products.**

Breakfast	QE	GF	MF	EF	SF	NF	PF	FF	SFF	V	VG	LFM
Aunt Ann's Baked Fresh Toast (p. 16)		X	P	P	P	X	X	X	X	X	P	
Baked Blueberry Coconut Oatmeal Crisp (p. 3)	X	X	X	X	X	X	X	X	X	X	X	P
Buckwheat Pancakes with Cinnamon Apples (p. 12)		X	P	X	X	X	X	X	X	X	P	

(continued)

Breakfast (*continued*)	QE	GF	MF	EF	SF	NF	PF	FF	SFF	V	VG	LFM
Cheese Blintzes with Fresh Strawberries and Whipped Cream (p. 10)		X		P	P	X	X	X	X	X		
Cranberry Almond Scones (p. 19)		X	P	P	X	P	X	X	X	X	P	P
Creamy Yogurt Shake (p. 18)	X	X	P	X	P	X	X	X	X	X	P	P
Parmesan Herb Egg Soufflé (p. 8)		X	P		P	X	X	X	X	X		P
Pumpkin Raisin Muffins with Pecan Streusel (p. 14)	X	X	P	P	P	P	X	X	X	X		
Sausage and Cheese Biscuits (p. 6)		X	P	X	X	X	X	X	X			P
Whole Grain Breakfast Cookies (p. 4)		X	P	P	P		X	X	X	X	P	

Starters

	QE	GF	MF	EF	SF	NF	PF	FF	SFF	V	VG	LFM
Arepa Sliders (p. 23)	X	X	P	X	X	X	X	X	X	P	P	X
Batter-Fried Onion Rings (p. 45)		X	P	P	X	X	X	X	X	X	P	

(continued)

Starters (continued)	QE	GF	MF	EF	SF	NF	PF	FF	SFF	V	VG	LFM
Bruschetta (p. 32)	X	X	P	P	P	X	X	X	X	X	P	P
Cheese Puffs (p. 34)		X	P	P	X	X	X	X	X	X	P	X
Cheesy Polenta Toasts with Roasted Mushrooms and Spinach (p. 43)		X	P	X	X	X	X	X	X	X	P	P
Crab Cakes (p. 25)	X	X	P	P	P	X	X	X				P
Crispy Zucchini Sticks (p. 41)	X	X	P	P	X	X	X	X	X	X		P
Crunchy Baked Chicken Tenders with Honey Mustard Dipping Sauce (p. 37)	X	X	P	X	P	X	X	X	X			X
Mini Knishes (p. 35)		X	X	P	X	X	X	X	X	X	P	X
Pigs in a Blanket (p. 36)		X	X	P	X	X	X	X	X			X
Pork Dumplings (p. 27)	X	X	X	X		X	X	X	X	P	P	P

(continued)

Starters (*continued*)	QE	GF	MF	EF	SF	NF	PF	FF	SFF	V	VG	LFM
Potato Pierogies (p. 39)		X		P	P	X	X	X	X	X		
Spring Rolls with Peanut Dipping Sauce (p. 29)	X	X	X	X	P	X	P	X	X	X	X	P

Salads, Sides, and Soups

	QE	GF	MF	EF	SF	NF	PF	FF	SFF	V	VG	LFM
Baked Sweet Potato Fries (p. 70)	X	X	X	X	P	X	X	X	X	X	X	P
Beef and Spinach Salad with Caramelized Shallots (p. 50)	X	X	P	X	X	X	X	X	X	P	P	P
Candied Carrots (p. 66)	X	X	P	X	X	X	X	X	X	X	P	P
Sweet Potatoes with Chipotle-Honey Glaze (p. 72)		X	X	X	X	X	X	X	X	X	P	P
Chopped Kale and Brussels Sprout Salad (p. 56)	X	X	X	X	X	X	X	X	X	X	X	

(continued)

Salads, Sides and Soups (continued)	QE	GF	MF	EF	SF	NF	PF	FF	SFF	V	VG	LFM
Creamed Spinach (p. 62)	X	X	P	X	P	X	X	X	X	X	P	P
Creamy Seafood Bisque (p. 73)		X	P	X	X	X	X					P
Creamy Yellow Split Pea and Sweet Potato Soup (p. 79)		X	X	X	X	P	X	X	X	X	X	P
Elbow Pasta with Broccoli and Cannellini Beans (p. 68)	X	X	P	X	X	X	X	X	X	P	P	P
Escarole and Beans (p. 59)	X	X	X	X	X	X	X	X	X	X	X	
French Onion Soup au Gratin (p. 75)		X	P	X	P	X	X	X	X	P	P	
Garlic Mashed Potatoes (p. 64)	X	X	P	X	P	X	X	X	X	X		P
Hearty Tuscan Soup with Meatballs (p. 77)		X	X	P	X	X	X	X	X			
Mediterranean Salad (p. 52)	X	X	P	X	X	X	X	X	X	X	P	P
Pineapple Coleslaw (p. 49)	X	X	X	P	P	X	X	X	X	X	P	
Rice Salad (p. 54)	X	X	X	X	X	P	X	X	X	X	X	P

(continued)

Salads, Sides and Soups (*continued*)	QE	GF	MF	EF	SF	NF	PF	FF	SFF	V	VG	LFM
Rice-Stuffed Tomatoes (p. 60)	X	X	X	X	X	X	X	X	X	X	X	P
Sautéed Garlic Green Beans (p. 67)	X	X	X	X	X	X	X	X	X	X	X	P
White Bean Salad (p. 57)	X	X	P	X	X	X	X	X	X	X	P	

Breads and Biscuits

	QE	GF	MF	EF	SF	NF	PF	FF	SFF	V	VG	LFM
French Bread (p. 88)		X	P	P	X	X	X	X	X	X	P	X
Garlic Knots (p. 94)		X	P	P	X	X	X	X	X	X	P	P
Irish Soda Bread (p. 86)		X	P	P	X	X	X	X	X	X	P	P
Naan (p. 82)		X	P	P	X	X	X	X	X	X	P	P
Pizza Dough (p. 95)		X	P	X	X	X	X	X	X	X	P	P
Potato Flatbread (p. 92)	X	X	X	P	X	X	X	X	X	X	P	X
Pull-Apart Rolls (p. 90)		X	P	P	X	P	X	X	X	X	P	P
Skillet Corn Cake (p. 84)	X	X	P	P	X	X	X	X	X	X	P	P

(continued)

Entrees	QE	GF	MF	EF	SF	NF	PF	FF	SFF	V	VG	LFM
Black Bean Burgers with Creamy Cilantro Pesto (p. 106)		X	P	P	X	X	X	X	X	X	P	
Chicken Cacciatore (p. 115)		X	X	X	P	X	X	X	X			P
Chicken Parmesan (p. 121)		X	P	P	P	X	X	X	X			P
Garlic Chicken (p. 111)		X	P	X	X	X	X	X	X			
Grilled Chicken with Spicy Mustard Sauce (p. 123)		X	P	P	P	X	X	X	X			P
Grilled Pork and Pineapple Kabobs (p. 109)		X	X	X		X	X	X	X			P
Grilled Salmon with Balsamic Glaze (p. 102)	X	X	X	X	X	X	X		X			P
Linguini with Turkey Bolognese (p. 119)		X	P	X	X	X	X	X	X			
Marinara Sauce (p. 117)		X	P	X	X	X	X	X	X	X	P	P

(continued)

Entrees (continued)	QE	GF	MF	EF	SF	NF	PF	FF	SFF	V	VG	LFM
Orange Roughy Piccatta (p. 104)	X	X	P	X	P	X	X		X			X
Quinoa Pasta with Chicken Tenders (p. 113)		X	P	X	P	X	X	X	X	P	P	
Sole Saint-Tropez (p. 99)	X	X	P	X	P	X	X		X			P
Tilapia with Salsa (p. 101)	X	X	X	X	X	X	X		X			

Sweets and Treats

	QE	GF	MF	EF	SF	NF	PF	FF	SFF	V	VG	LFM
Almond Cherry Tart (p. 146)		X	P	P	X	P	X	X	X	X	P	
Apple Crumb Pie (p. 142)		X	P	X	X	P	X	X	X	X	P	
Aunt Louise and Eileen's Cheesecake (p. 129)		X		P	X	X	X	X	X	X		
Black and White Cookies (p. 131)		X	P	P	X	P	X	X	X	X	P	P
Cannoli Cones (p. 134)	X	X		X	P	X	X	X	X	X		
Carrot Cake with Creamy Cream Cheese Frosting (p. 163)		X		P	P		X	X	X	X		P

(continued)

Sweets and Treats (continued)	QE	GF	MF	EF	SF	NF	PF	FF	SFF	V	VG	LFM
Cashew Butter Truffles (p. 145)	X	X	P	X	X		X	X	X	X	P	
Cherry Vanilla Chip Shortbread (p. 159)		X		X		X	X	X	X	X		
Chocolate Covered Macaroons (p. 149)	X	X	P	P	P	P	X	X	X	X	P	
Chocolate Peanut Butter Tart (p. 127)		X		X			X	X	X	P	P	
Cinnamon Sugar Cookies (p. 155)		X	P	P	P	X	X	X	X	X	P	P
Cream Puffs (p. 140)		X	P	P	X	X	X	X	X	X	P	
Double Peanut Butter Chocolate Chunk Cookies (p. 157)		X		P			X	X	X			
Peach Cobbler (p. 135)		X	P	P	X	P	X	X	X	X	P	P
Popcorn Balls (p. 144)	X	X	P	X	X	X	P	X	X	X	P	X
Pumpkin Tart with Bourbon Whipped Cream (p. 152)		X	P	P	X	P	X	X	X	X	P	X

(continued)

Sweets and Treats (*continued*)	QE	GF	MF	EF	SF	NF	PF	FF	SFF	V	VG	LFM
Rocky Road (p. 151)	X	X	P	X	P			X	X	X	P	
Salted Caramel–Filled Fudge Cupcakes with Brown Sugar Frosting (p. 161)		X				X	X	X	X	X		
Sweet Potato Pie (p. 137)		X	P	P	X	P	X	X	X	X	P	P
Tres Leches Flan Cake (p. 165)		X				X	X	X	X	X		

Cooking for a Crowd

	QE	GF	MF	EF	SF	NF	PF	FF	SFF	V	VG	LFM
Braised Short Ribs (p. 188)		X	X	X	X	X	X	X	X			
Chicken with Mushrooms and Cream Sauce (p. 184)		X	P	X	X	X	X	X	X			
Brisket with Cranberry-Chili Glaze (p. 174)		X	X	X	X	X	X	X	X			
Hawaiian Chicken (p. 182)		X	X	X	P	X	X	X	X			
Holiday Ham with Pineapple Glaze (p. 172)		X	X	X	X	X	X	X	X			

(*continued*)

Cooking for a Crowd (*continued*)	QE	GF	MF	EF	SF	NF	PF	FF	SFF	V	VG	LFM
Lemon Chicken (p. 178)	X	X	P	X	X	X	X	X	X			P
Linguini with Shrimp and Petite Diced Tomatoes (p. 180)		X	P	X	X	X	X	X				P
Macaroni and Cheese (p. 186)		X		X	X	X	X	X	X	X		
Oven-Baked "Fried" Chicken (p. 192)		X	P	X	X	X	X	X	X			P
Rosemarie's Pasta with Sun-Dried Tomatoes and Sausage Bolognese (p. 169)		X			X		X	X	X			
Stir-Fried Rice Noodles with Peanuts (p. 176)	X	X	X	X		X		X	X	X	X	P
Turkey Meat Loaf (p. 190)	X	X	X	P	X	X	X	X	X			P

(continued)

One-Dish Dinners	QE	GF	MF	EF	SF	NF	PF	FF	SFF	V	VG	LFM
Broccoli and Cheese Casserole (p. 195)		X		X	X	X	X	X	X	X		
Chickpeas with Butternut Squash and Spinach (p. 197)		X	X	X	X	X	X	X	X	X	X	
Deep-Dish Chicken Pot Pie (p. 214)		X	P	X	X	X	X	X	X			
Eggplant and Rice Casserole (p. 199)		X		X	X	X	X	X	X	P		
Homemade Cheese Ravioli (p. 207)		X			X	X	X	X	X	X		
Homemade Manicotti (p. 203)		X		P	X	X	X	X	X	X		
Pasta e Fagioli (p. 211)		X		X	X	X	X	X	X			
Shepherd's Pie (p. 209)		X		X	X	X	X	X	X			P
Shrimp Risotto (p. 201)		X	P	X	X	X	X	X				P
Slow-Cooked White Chicken Chili (p. 205)		X	P	X	X	X	X	X	X			
Turkey a la King (p. 213)	X	X		X	X	X	X	X	X			

Index

About the Author

MARLISA BROWN MS, RD, CDE, CDN, is a registered dietitian, certified diabetes educator, chef, author, and international speaker. She has served as president of Total Wellness, Inc., for over 20 years, and works as a nutritional consultant specializing in diabetes education, celiac disease, gastrointestinal disorders, cardiovascular disease, sports nutrition, culinary programs, and corporate wellness. She has coordinated corporate wellness programs, nutritional menu selections, and promotions with the New York Jets, Kennedy Space Center, Pratt and Whitney, Honeywell, Hofstra and Adelphi universities, Lilco, Guardian Life, Brookhaven National Laboratory, Goldman Sachs, Dean Witter Reynolds, Pall Corporation, Bank of New York, Sony, Liz Claiborne, Ethicon, and more. Brown worked for 10 years as the welllness coordinator for Lackmann Culinary Services, coordinating wellness and marketing programs, implementing their "Lighter by Choice" program, and developing recipes.

Brown is co-owner of MCSeminars (MCSeminars.org) a professional presentation company specializing in marketing, business skills, health care, and culinary programs. She has been a regular speaker for PESI Healthcare since 2011, providing programs on obesity, food allergies, gluten-free diets, and diabetes.

She is the author of *Gluten-Free, Hassle Free* and the *American Dietetic Association Easy Gluten-Free* (with Tricia Thompson, MS, RD), and has contributed to many dietary programs and books, including Richard Simmons's *The Food Mover* program, Jorge Cruise's cookbook *The 3 Hour Diet*, Leslie Sansone's *Walk Away the Pounds*, and Kathy Smith's *Project: YOU! Type 2*. Brown has contributed to many publications including *Salute, Scholastic, Shape, Food Service Management, Newsday, Parenting,* and *Today's Dietitian*.

With over 30 years' culinary experience, she has been featured in over 50 cooking shows for the American Heart Association on International Cooking. Brown is on the Board of Directors for the Long Island chapter of The Gluten-Intolerance Group of North America and is past chair of The International Association of Culinary Professionals nutrition section. She is also on the advisory panel for *Today's Dietitian* as a gluten expert. A member of the National Speakers Association, she has served as the past president of the New York State Dietetic Association and nominating chair for Dietitians for Integrative and Functional Medicine.

Brown has been the recipient of the following awards: "2011 Diabetes Educator of the Year" from The American Dietetic Association's Diabetes

Care DPG; "1996 Emerging Dietetic Leader" from The American Dietetic Association; "2008 Dietitian of the Year" from The Long Island Dietetic Association; "Best Nutritionist" 2008/2009/2010/2011 from *The Long Island Press*; and "1994 The Community Service Award" from CW Post Long Island University.

Brown has a BS in Marketing and MS in Nutrition from CW Post Long Island University and is currently listed on the university's website as an outstanding alumna. She has also studied at the Culinary Institute of America.

Visit her blog at www.glutenfreeez.com

Printed in the United States
By Bookmasters